Binger Hermann

Louisiana Purchase and Our Title West of the Rocky Mountains

With a Review of Annexation by the United States

Binger Hermann

Louisiana Purchase and Our Title West of the Rocky Mountains
With a Review of Annexation by the United States

ISBN/EAN: 9783337317454

Printed in Europe, USA, Canada, Australia, Japan

Cover: Foto ©ninafisch / pixelio.de

More available books at **www.hansebooks.com**

LOUISIANA PURCHASE

AND

OUR TITLE WEST OF THE ROCKY
MOUNTAINS,

WITH

A REVIEW OF ANNEXATION BY THE UNITED STATES.

BY

BINGER HERMANN,
COMMISSIONER OF THE GENERAL LAND OFFICE.

WASHINGTON:
GOVERNMENT PRINTING OFFICE.
1898.

SYNOPSIS.

THE LOUISIANA PURCHASE.
  Error in United States map.
  What was the original Louisiana?.
    LaSalle's descent of the Mississippi.
    LaSalle takes possession in name of Louis XIV.
    DeTonty's narrative of the discovery.
    Iberville's exploration of the mouth of the Mississippi.
    Settlement at Biloxi.
    Spanish claim to territory along Gulf east of Mississippi.
    De Soto at Tampa Bay.
    First settlement of New Orleans.
    The grant to Crozat.
    Moll's map.
    Bowen's map of North America.
    Jefferson's letter to Mellish.
    Franquelin's map.
    Crozat's colony abandoned.
FRANCE CEDES TO SPAIN.
  Treaty between France and Spain.
  Louisiana a troublesome and expensive province.
    De Ulloa's arrival at New Orleans.
    His expulsion.
    Spanish fleet appears before New Orleans.
SPAIN CEDES FLORIDA TO GREAT BRITAIN.
  Confusing treaties.
    The family compact.
    Talleyrand's explanation.
THE FLORIDAS RETROCEDED TO SPAIN.
THE UNITED STATES AND SPAIN.
  Southern boundary defined.
  American settlements.
    The navigation of the Mississippi.
  Popular discontent.
  Attempts to secure commercial privileges.
SPAIN RETROCEDES TO FRANCE.
  The treaty of San Ildefonso, 1800.
  Depredations upon our commerce by France.
    Preparations to resent such depredations.
  Dismissal of our envoys.

SYNOPSIS.

	Page.
...IN RETROCEDES TO FRANCE—Continued.	
Livingston's remarks	26
Threatened war between France and England	27
Monroe nominated for an extraordinary mission to France.	27
New Orleans and Florida are demanded	28
Napoleon offers to cede all of Louisiana	28
Two prominent actors	29
Thomas Jefferson	29
Marquis de Marbois	29
The American negotiators	30
Robert R. Livingston	30
James Monroe	30
LOUISIANA CEDED TO THE UNITED STATES	32
Indefinite boundaries	32
Ratifications exchanged	33
Possession taken	34
A rivalry for honor	35
Livingston's letter	35
The magnitude of the purchase	36
Its population in 1890	36
Statistics	36
Early opposition to annexation	36
Speeches in Congress adverse to cession	37
A striking contrast	38
VALUE AND RESOURCES OF LOUISIANA PURCHASE	38
Colorado:	
Its gold, silver and cattle	38
Wyoming:	
Its cattle and sheep	38
Montana:	
Its silver, copper, cattle and sheep	38
South Dakota:	
Its gold and wheat	39
North Dakota:	
Its wheat	39
Oklahoma:	
Its wheat and cotton	39
Its wonderful development	39
THE LEWIS AND CLARKE EXPEDITION	39
Jefferson's object was to secure trade relations	41
THE FLORIDA BOUNDARIES UNCERTAIN	42
The United States dispossesses Spain	45
The Florida wars	47
The Florida treaty	47
OUR WESTERN LIMIT OF LOUISIANA	48
La Salle's settlement	48
THE ANNEXATION OF TEXAS	48
Its value and resources	48
Cotton and live stock	49
OUR NATION CLAIMS BEYOND THE ROCKIES	49
The claims of England	49
The claims of Spain	50
England's claim contested	51
RUSSIA'S CLAIM ACKNOWLEDGED	51
Russia sells Alaska to the United States	52

SYNOPSIS.

	Page.
Russia's Claim Acknowledged—Continued.	
Opposition to the purchase	52
Speeches in Congress adverse thereto	52
The value and resources of Alaska	53
Its gold production	53
The fish of Alaska	54
The fur seals	54
Joint Occupancy and Negotiation	55
The British ultimatum	55
The mystery of the forty-ninth parallel	55
No evidence adopting the forty-ninth parallel	56
Hall J. Kelley's immigration scheme	60
The Wilkes Exploring Expedition	61
American settlements encouraged	62
"Fifty-four, Forty, or Fight"	62
Our northern boundary defined	63
Oregon Admitted as a Territory	63
The question of slavery	63
Thomas H. Benton	65
Oregon provisional government	65
The pioneers of the West	65
The extent of the Oregon country	66
A splendid empire	67
Its value and resources	67
Oregon:	
Its gold, live stock, wheat and other products	67
Washington:	
Its timber, wheat and live stock	68
Idaho:	
Its gold, silver and live stock	68
Our Mexican Purchase	68
Its extent	69
California:	
Its gold, wheat, live stock, hay, lumber, barley, wine and fruits	69
The Gold Product of the United States	69
The Silver Product of the United States for 1896	70
Utah:	
Its gold, silver, live stock and wheat	69
Nevada:	
Its gold, silver and live stock	69
New Mexico:	
Its cattle, sheep and wheat	69
Arizona:	
Its gold, copper, cattle and sheep	70
Total cost of annexations	70
Imperfect statistics	70
Oregon and the Louisiana Purchase	70
The claim of contiguity	72
Sir Alexander McKenzie's expedition	74
No proof that Oregon was included in the Louisiana purchase	75
Authorities cited	75
Official declarations increased popular error	75
Jefferson, Marbois, and Greenhow	76
Conclusions and recommendations	78

SYNOPSIS.

	Page.
A REVIEW OF ANNEXATION BY THE UNITED STATES	79
Early objections to annexation analyzed	79
The extent of our acquisitions	79
Remoteness	79
The constitutionality of annexation	80
Annexation an element of strength	81
Homogeneity not a serious objection	81
Annexation by other nations and their foreign elements	82
An object lesson in England's assimilation of races	83
Our further destiny	84
Our increasing commerce	84
Hawaii	85
Our Asiatic trade	85
The Sandwich Islands a safeguard	86
The Nicaragua Canal	86

ILLUSTRATIONS.

Territorial growth of the United States.... .... Frontispiece.

	Before page
Map by Franquelin in 1684	13
Moll's map, 1710	15
Map of Alaska	52
Map of Hawaiian Islands	85
Thomas Jefferson in 1803	29
Barbé Marbois	29
Robert R. Livingston	30
President Monroe	31
William H. Seward	55
President Polk	63
Thomas H. Benton	65

DEPARTMENT OF THE INTERIOR,
GENERAL LAND OFFICE,
Washington, July 7, 1898.

SIR: I have the honor to submit herewith my recommendation for a correction of the last published map of the United States by the Department, so far as it represents the portion of our country westward of the Rocky Mountains and now embracing Oregon, Washington, Idaho and portions of Montana and Wyoming to have been acquired by the United States by or through the Louisiana Purchase, the correction to be made in the republication of that map by the Department; and in connection with such recommendation I respectfully submit various conclusions which I have reached relating to this subject, including a review of the various annexations by the United States, which I hope will meet your approval.

Very respectfully,

BINGER HERMANN,
Commissioner.

Hon. CORNELIUS N. BLISS,
Secretary of the Interior.

DEPARTMENT OF THE INTERIOR,
Washington, July 8, 1898.

SIR: Your letter of the 7th instant has been received. You call attention therein to an error in the last map of the United States published by the Department (1897) in so far as it represents the portion of the country westward of the Rocky Mountains now embracing Oregon, Washington, Idaho and portions of Montana and Wyoming to have been acquired by the United States by or through the Louisiana Purchase. You also submit in connection therewith a very carefully prepared paper upon the matter of the Louisiana Purchase, and upon the various annexations made by the United States, and recommend that the error in question be corrected upon the next map of the United States to be published by the Department.

Upon careful consideration of the matter, as so ably presented by you, your recommendations in the premises meet with my approval, and the correction will be made upon the next map of the United States to be issued by the Department.

Very respectfully,

C. N. BLISS,
Secretary.

Hon. BINGER HERMANN,
Commissioner of the General Land Office.

THE LOUISIANA PURCHASE

AND

OUR TITLE WEST OF THE ROCKY MOUNTAINS,

WITH

A REVIEW OF ANNEXATION BY THE UNITED STATES.

By BINGER HERMANN,
Commissioner of the General Land Office.

Of all distinguishing events in the glorious career of this country, aside from its triumphs for liberty and for union, none shine forth with such imperishable luster as the acquisition of that splendid empire west of the Mississippi River; and when the impartial historian shall write up the great men and the great measures of our nation he will place at the top of the rolls Thomas Jefferson and the Louisiana Purchase. The importance, then, of this subject deserves that it shall be accurately as well as impartially reviewed.

I am induced to enter upon this matter because of an error which I conceive exists upon the map of the United States as published under the direction of my predecessor, and which goes forth with the official indorsement of the Department. The error to which I refer is in the representation that the cession of Louisiana from France in 1803 comprised territory west of the Rocky Mountains, now known as Oregon, Washington, Idaho and portions of Montana and Wyoming. Believing that such domain was derived by the United States based on the right of discovery, exploration and occupancy by our own people, together with the cession from Spain, by treaty of February 22, 1819, of such adverse rights as that nation claimed to possess, I have assumed the liberty of representing these facts on the new edition of the United States map soon to be published by the Department.

In support of this position I submit the conclusions to which I have arrived, together with the views of eminent historians, diplomats, statesmen and writers on both sides of this interesting and famous contention. In subsequent pages I shall refer to the value of this acquisition and to the advantages which have followed our other annexations to the public domain.

WHAT WAS THE ORIGINAL LOUISIANA?

First, it may be asked, what was originally understood to be the Louisiana territory? It is essential that we know the extent of this domain as it was understood by the men who discovered, explored and named it, and then described it to the world.

La Salle was the first to descend the Mississippi from its navigable northern waters to its mouth, and from the Gulf inward again. His discovery was not a mere accident, nor was it left unwritten and in doubt. His journey was undertaken for purposes of discovery, and every important observation was carefully noted and reported by him. He was a man of education and received a patent of nobility. His expeditions were under the authority of the French Government, and he early won the confidence and admiration of that nation's monarch, Louis XIV. The Chevalier Henry de Tonty, Fathers Hennepin and Membre and other well-known explorers were his companions in many expeditions, and a few years before, over much of the same ground, Marquette and Joliet had opened the way among the Indian tribes. The result of his researches was made known in France, and efforts were at once made by the government to colonize the country and extend exploration.

La Salle, standing with Tonty, Dautray and other companions on the banks of the most western channel of the Mississippi, about 3 leagues from its mouth, on April 9, 1682, took possession of the country in the name of Louis XIV, and setting up a column, or, as Dr. Kohl insists, "a cross with arms of the King," buried a plate, unfurled the flag of France, sung a Te Deum and naming the country "Louisiana" in a loud voice, proclaimed its extent to be "from the mouth of the great river St. Louis, on the eastern side, otherwise called Ohio, Alighin, Sipore, or Chiskagona, and this with the consent of the Chaonanons, Chikachas and other people dwelling therein with whom we have made alliance, as also along the river Colbert, or Mississippi and rivers which discharge themselves therein, from its source beyond the Kious or Nadonessions, and this with their consent, and with the consent of the Motanties, Illinois, Mesigameus, Natches, Koroas, which are the most considerable nations dwelling therein, with whom also we have made alliance * * * as far as its mouth at the sea or Gulf of Mexico * * * and also to the mouth of the river Palms, upon the assurance which we have received from all these nations that we are the first Europeans who have descended or ascended the said river Colbert."

He also named the Mississippi "Colbert," in honor of his friend and patron, M. Colbert, the colonial minister under Louis XIV, and upon whose report the King conferred upon La Salle the rank of esquire, with power to acquire knighthood.

De Tonty, La Salle's companion, who has written a detailed narrative of the discovery, describes the countries at the heads of the various tributaries of the Mississippi, all of which were included under the name of "Louisiana," and it is remarkable how accurately he estimates the distance of one river from another

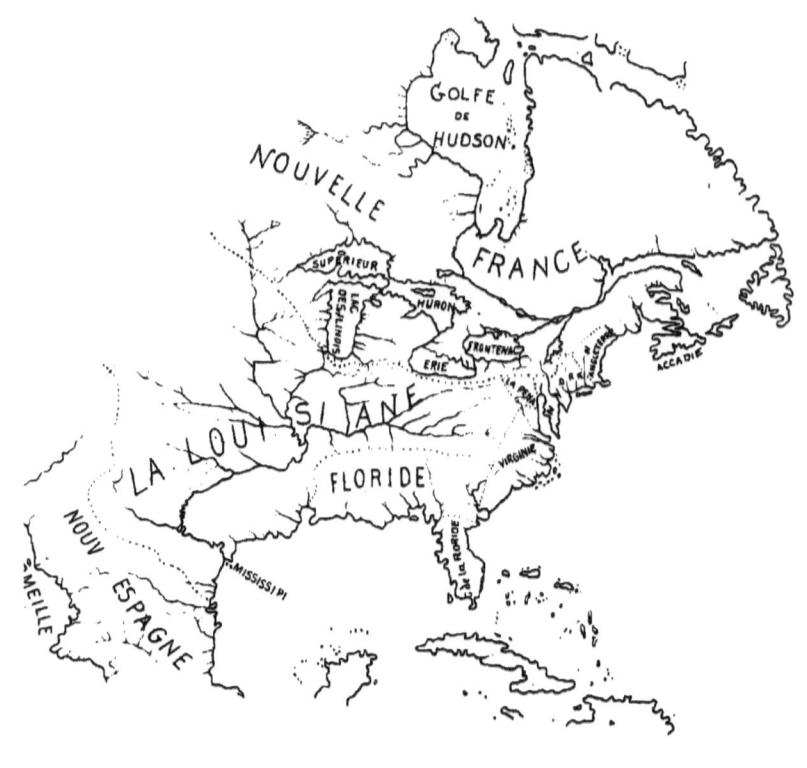

MAP OF FRANQUELIN 1684.

and the length of each. The Falls of St. Anthony seem to have been known, as Hennepin was sent by La Salle to that point, and the Missouri from its source is mentioned and described at different points. A map prepared by De Tonty, as he states, accompanied his report and exhibited the general scope of country embraced within Louisiana. Unfortunately nothing more is known of this map. No reference, however, was ever made to any country westward of the highlands which are the sources of the rivers flowing from the west into the Mississippi; and Louisiana was never understood as extending beyond those highlands by any of these explorers. This is further corroborated by Franquelin, a young French engineer, who was in Quebec when La Salle returned from his discovery, and who learned from him the extent of the same, and then crudely mapped the country on what has since been known as Franquelin's Great Map of 1684, on which is shown Louisiana with the western boundary on the head waters of the Mississippi.

On March 2, 1699, Iberville, a daring French explorer, entered the mouth of the Mississippi and ascended 100 leagues, and on descending passed through the river Iberville, named for him, and thence through lakes Maurepas and Pontchartrain into the Gulf. The last-named lake was named by Iberville in honor of the Count de Pontchartrain, who was minister of marine under Louis XIV. The former lake was named after Count Maurepas, minister under Louis XV and Louis XVI, and who died with the ill-fated King.

The land westward of these waterways and eastward of the Mississippi from the island of New Orleans, being a part of the French discoveries, is properly included in Louisiana. In 1721 French immigrants arrived at Mobile Bay and at Biloxi, and previous to this the French Canadian, Du Tissenet, with an escort, went from Dauphine Island by way of Mobile river to Quebec. The first colony was settled at Biloxi in 1699. It was for some time the chief settlement of Louisiana, and contained a fort.

To the east of the Mississippi, Franquelin has shown Florida with a dotted boundary which was then much as it is at present, except that for some distance east of the Mississippi the country then was included in Louisiana. The map is also evidence of the presence of the Spaniards, and La Salle in his memorials presented to the King his scheme of erecting fortifications near the mouths of the Mississippi and then of driving out the neighboring Spanish colonists. Here we have at the very outset material for the subsequent disputes as to West Florida, and the uncertainty as to whether it was French in the Louisiana claim or Florida under prior Spanish discovery. At this point it may be as well to inquire into the claim of the Spaniards as to that territory along the Gulf east of the Mississippi. Commencing with Ponce de Leon, who reached the coast of Florida near the present site of St. Augustine March 27, 1512, we next find Miruelo, who arrived from Cuba in 1516; then De Cordova, who arrived in 1517 with an expedition of Spaniards who were seeking gold ; and he was followed by Alaminos with several ships for the same purpose. In 1539 we find Hernando de Soto landing with a large company of Spaniards at Tampa Bay, and from there he went to Tallahassee;

THE LOUISIANA PURCHASE.

thence he moved to the Savannah River below the present site of Augusta, and then toward the head of Mobile Bay, and then to the Mississippi, which he discovered near the mouth of the Arkansas. After his death, near the mouth of Red river, his successor, Luis de Moscoso, took the command, numbering about 300, down the Mississippi to the Gulf, July 18, 1543.

In 1528 De Narvaez led a large force of Spaniards and landed in Clear Water Bay, following along the Gulf shore on the west. A portion returned to Cuba, while the greater portion were destroyed. None made settlement. Still further east on the Florida coast French colonies were founded, but these were driven out in 1563 by Menendez with Spanish troops, who then erected forts from St. Augustine northward as far as Carolina. This possession was maintained to the time when La Salle claimed Louisiana for France. It may be said of the Spaniards, however, that they made no attempt to gain a foothold far in the interior, and this explains the narrow limit of their possession north from the Gulf. Bienville was appointed governor of Louisiana in 1717, and one of his first acts in that year was to select a principal establishment for the French colony, which he did by choosing the site which is now the city of New Orleans. It was then covered by a dense forest, the soil being swampy. A detachment of soldiers was left there for the double purpose of clearing the ground and of protecting the colonists. This was the origin of New Orleans, named in honor of the Duke of Orleans, the then regent of France. In 1723 the seat of government was definitely removed to that place, which then contained 300 population. It is worthy of notice at this point that in this year the French Government considered the importance of securing deeper water at the entrance to the Mississippi, and that the official engineer—Pauger—had recommended a plan of improvement which was in principle based largely on the modern jetty system.

On September 14, 1712, a grant was made by Louis XIV to Antoine de Crozat, a rich merchant of Paris, for trading purposes. The King in this grant says:

* * * we did in the year 1683 give our orders to undertake a discovery of the countries and lands which are situated in the northern part of America, between New France and New Mexico; and the Sieur de la Salle, to whom we committed that enterprise, having had success enough to confirm a belief that communication might be settled from New France to the Gulf of Mexico, by means of large rivers; this obliged us, immediately after the peace of Ryswick, to give orders for the establishing of a colony there, and maintaining a garrison, which has kept and preserved the possession we had taken in the very year 1683, of the lands, coasts, and islands, which are situated in the Gulf of Mexico, between Carolina on the east, and Old and New Mexico on the west. * * * And whereas, upon the information we have received, concerning the disposition and situation of the said countries, known at present by the name of the province of Louisiana, we are of opinion that there may be established therein a considerable commerce * * * we have resolved to grant the commerce of the country of Louisiana to the sieur Anthony Crozat.

The further language of this grant sheds more light in identifying the limits of this province in these words:

and do appoint the said sieur Crozat, solely to carry on a trade in all the lands, possessed by us, and bounded by New Mexico, and by the lands of the English Carolina, * * * the river of

St. Lewis, heretofore called Mississippi, from the edge of the sea, as far as the Illinois, tog... or with the river of St. Philip, heretofore called the Missourys, * *   with all the countries & territories, lakes within land, and the rivers which fall directly or indirectly into that part of the river St. Lewis.

1. Our pleasure is that all the aforesaid lands, streams, rivers and islands, be and remain comprised under the name of the government of Louisiana, which shall be dependent upon the general government of New France, * * * *

A map published about 1710 by Moll, the English geographer, represents Louisiana to be as Louis XIV describes it. To the east and along the Gulf coast the country containing the Carolinas is marked as British Empire. On the west, as a boundary, is New Mexico and Old Mexico, while on the north is New France, Lake Huron, and Upper Lake (Superior). A portion of the western boundary is shown as the "North River" (Del Norte river). The more northwestern boundaries are represented by the highlands at the sources of the Mississippi and the Missouri, marked on the map, respectively, as the rivers St. Louis and St. Philip. Nothing west of the Rocky Mountains is designated as Louisiana, and all north of California is marked as "Unknown Parts."

In a later map, and before 1762, published by Thomas Bowen, entitled "An accurate map of North America from the best authorities," the country north of Cape Blanco (on the Oregon coast) is marked as "Unknown," while that east of the Rio del Norte and the Rocky Mountains, and the country drained by the waters of the Missouri and Mississippi and as far east as the "Apalachan Mountains" is marked as Louisiana, while Florida, Georgia, Carolina, Virginia and Pennsylvania, to the east of these mountains, are all excluded from the boundaries of Louisiana. This map will be found in Brooks's Gazetteer, 1st edition, 1762. As showing Jefferson's knowledge as to what constituted Louisiana, his letter to Mellish, the geographer, is submitted, as follows:

MONTICELLO, *December 31, 1816.*

To Mr. MELLISH.

SIR, Your favor of November 23d, after a very long passage, is received, and with it the map which you have been so kind as to send me, for which I return you many thanks. It is handsomely executed, and on a well chosen scale; giving a luminous view of the comparative possession of different powers in our America. It is on account of the value I set on it, that I will make some suggestions.

By the charter of Louis XIV. all the country comprehending the waters which flow into the Mississippi, was made a part of Louisiana. Consequently its northern boundary was the summit of the highlands in which its northern waters rise.

But by the Xth Art. of the Treaty of Utrecht, France and England agreed to appoint commissioners to settle the boundary between their possessions in that quarter, and those commissioners settled it at the 49th degree of latitude. See Hutchinson's Topographical Description of Louisiana, p. 7. This it was which induced the British Commissioners, in settling the boundary with us, to follow the northern water line to the Lake of the Woods, at the latitude of 49°, and then go off on that parallel. This, then, is the true northern boundary of Louisiana.

The western boundary of Louisiana is, rightfully, the Rio Bravo, (its main stream,) from its mouth to its source, and thence along the highlands and mountains dividing the waters of the Mississippi from those of the Pacific. The usurpations of Spain on the east side of that river, have induced geographers to suppose the Puerco or Salado to be the boundary. The line along the highlands stands on the charter of Louis XIV. that of the Rio Bravo, on the circumstance that, when La Salle took possession of the Bay of St. Bernard, Panuco w... the nearest possession of Spain, and the Rio Bravo the natural half way boundary between them.

On the waters of the Pacific, we can found no cl... im in right of Louisiana. If we claim that country at all, it must be on Astor's settlement near the mouth of the Columbia, and the principle of the *ius gentium* of America, that when a civilized nation takes possession of the mouth of a river in a new country, that possession is considered as including all its waters.

The line of latitude of the southern source of the Multnomat might be claimed as appurtenant to Astoria. For its northern boundary, I believe an understanding has been come to between our government and Russia, which might be known from some of its members. I do not know it.

Although the irksomeness of writing, which you may perceive from the present letter, and its labor, oblige me now to withdraw from letter writing, yet the wish that your map should set to rights the ideas of our own countrymen, as well as foreign nations, as to our correct boundaries, has induced me to make these suggestions, that you may bestow on them whatever inquiry they may merit.

I salute you with esteem and respect.

Perhaps the most noted map of this period is that by the French engineer, Louis Franquelin, previously mentioned herein, which was published as early as 1684, following the possession by France; and there is outlined on this map the boundaries of Louisiana nearly as claimed by Louis XIV, and these limits were justified by the recognized authority of those days, which gave to the discoverer of the mouth of a river the whole country drained by it.

Justin Winsor, in his Narrative and Critical History of America, in commenting on that law as applied to the discovery of the Mississippi, says:

By this the French claim was bounded by the Gulf of Mexico westward to the Rio Grande; thence northward to the rather vague watershed of what we now know as the Rocky Mountains, with an indefinite line along the source of the Upper Mississippi and its higher affluents, bounding on the height of land which shut off the valley of the Great Lakes until the Appalachians were reached. Following these mountains south, the line skirted the northern limits of Spanish Florida, and then turned to the Gulf. * * At the north the head waters of the great river were still unknown, and long to remain so.

The province which was granted to Crozat was by him surrendered back September 6, 1717, and his colony abandoned. The same year another grant was made to the Mississippi Commercial Company, under the regency of the Duke of Orleans. This was the celebrated John Law's Mississippi scheme. This charter was later on also surrendered. This, then, was the original and only Louisiana, and it is seen that no country is included west of the Rocky Mountains. France claimed nothing beyond, and the country known as Louisiana was recognized by the bounds already mentioned. For nearly eighty years following La Salle's discovery the country named by him as Louisiana remained intact as French possessions; but its dismemberment and change of sovereignty was near at hand. If this territory was Louisiana, as we thus far understood the boundaries, and such as France had claimed, could it not be contended to be the same Louisiana that was ceded to Spain? Was it not Spanish domain from the moment the cession was signed and ratified? A study of the treaties, however, which are to follow, will convey that territory to different sovereignties.

FRANCE CEDES TO SPAIN.

The treaty between France and Spain of November 3, 1762, was the first move in change of sovereignty. In that treaty the granting words are:

his Most Christian Majesty cedes in entire possession, purely and simply, without exception, to his Catholic Majesty and his successors in perpetuity, all the country known under the name of Louisiana, as well as New Orleans and the island in which that place stands.

This was made subject to the later approval and acceptance of the Spanish King. On the 13th of the same month the acceptance was made final.

This treaty between the two monarchs was never known publicly in the United States until seventy years after, and until published, in 1837, in the appendix to Gales & Seaton's Reports of Debates, Twenty-fourth Congress, second session, volume 13. This will account for the misunderstanding among so many of our public men in the time of Jefferson's administration as to the exact territory which belonged to either France or Spain.

The orders for the surrender of Louisiana, with New Orleans and the island, were not issued at Versailles until April 21, 1764.

By reference to the treaty it will be observed that the cession to Spain merely refers to the transfer as "the country known under the name of Louisiana, together with New Orleans and the island on which that city stands." There is no other description or designation. Whether Spain claimed Florida west to the Iberville, or how far north along the Mississippi, and north of the thirty-first degree of latitude, or how far France claimed for Louisiana east of the Iberville, or anything between the Mississippi and the Florida country—all these were matters of uncertainty and contention. By another move at the same time this uncertainty was attempted to be cleared. The cession to Spain of Louisiana was accompanied, or, it should more properly be said, was followed, by the adjustment and agreement known in history as the Treaty of Paris, which was concluded February 10, 1763, between Great Britain and Portugal on the one part, and Spain and France on the other, in which France ceded to Great Britain Nova Scotia (or Acadia), Canada with all its dependencies, the island of Cape Breton and also all the other islands and coasts on the Gulf and River St. Lawrence. The same treaty further fixed the boundary or confines between the British and French possessions by a "line drawn along the middle of the river Mississippi, from its source to the river Iberville, and from thence by a line drawn along the middle of this river, and the lakes Maurepas and Pontchartrain, to the sea," and then the treaty makes to Great Britain still another cession: "the river and port of Mobile, and everything which he possesses, or ought to possess, on the left side of the river Mississippi, except the town of New Orleans and the island in which it is situated, which shall remain to France." There was an important clause in the treaty which later gave rise to much misunderstanding wherein it was "provided that the navigation of the river Mississippi shall be equally free, as well to the subjects of Great Britain as to those of France, in its whole breadth and length, from its source to the sea, and expressly that part which is between the said island of New Orleans and the right bank of that river, as well as the passage both in and out of its mouth. It is further stipulated; that the vessels belonging to the subjects of either nation shall not be stopped, visited or subjected to the payment of any duty whatever."

LOUISIANA A TROUBLESOME AND EXPENSIVE PROVINCE.

Louisiana had been a source of infinite trouble and expense to France. From the first effort at colonization, insubordination, discord and malfeasance among those in authority continued to exist, while the maintenance of troops and the expensive contributions of merchandise constantly made to the Indian tribes in proximity (who demanded such supplies as a condition of peace with the colonists and of their alliance in time of conflict against the English), were all very costly to the home government. The colony had proven in all things to be very unprofitable. Crozat, the rich and calculating merchant, found it to be a loss even as a present, and he gladly relinquished his grant. The India or Law Company lost twenty millions in expensive schemes to develop a commerce under its chartered privileges. It is conceded that the French government squandered over forty millions of livres in colonization efforts in Louisiana. It was such discouragements as made France willing and anxious to cede to Spain all her interest in such possessions, and to release herself from the further obligation of bearing an increasing financial burden. The transfer to Spain was delayed until after the portion east of the Mississippi had been surrendered to the English. It was this delay which led the French colonists west of the river to hope that they would continue to remain on French territory. The official notice of Louis XV, dated April 21, 1764, to the French governor, D'Abbadie, and received in October, 1764, to deliver possession to the Spaniards, dispelled all further hope of the colonists, and they submitted with indignation and humiliation. It was not, however, until March 5, 1766, that the Spanish governor, Antonio de Ulloa, with two companies of infantry, arrived at New Orleans. He had intended to defer taking complete possession until the arrival of the Spanish troops. He met, to his surprise, a sullen reception from the citizens, though he had achieved great renown before the world. He was an eminent scholar and writer, and a famous sailor, having attained the grade of lieutenant-general of the royal navies of Spain. Few men at the time of his death had contributed so much to the general knowledge and scientific advancement of a nation as De Ulloa. The knowledge of platina, of electricity, of artificial magnetism, of engraving and printing, was greatly advanced by the researches of this man. He was also a great promoter of astronomy. In Spain the credit is given him of having discovered the secret of manufacturing superfine cloth by a combination of the churla wool with the merino; and in this connection he founded at Segovia, in Spain, a manufactory where cloths of remarkable fineness were produced. He was a benefactor of his race and of his time. Looking back upon that remote period in the history of Louisiana and upon its wild and undeveloped state, we may well marvel that one so famed among his countrymen should have consented to so exile himself as to become the first governor under Spanish rule of that distant and distracted colony. The inhabitants, however, could not forget that they were French, and they resented the act of cession which transferred them and their territory to another flag and another nationality without their acquiescence and in defiance of their repeated protests. They could not become reconciled, however distinguished and excellent the Spanish governor who was to represent the changed sovereignty. The discontent manifested itself at first in assemblages of the people, who denounced the treaty of cession. This was followed by open revolution. De Ulloa was forced to seek safety in the Spanish ship which lay at anchor in the harbor. The limited military force was powerless to protect the governor, although Aubry, the French governor-general of the colony under the French authority, exerted every influence in his power loyally and fearlessly to execute the mandate of his sovereign—the French King—in making effective the cession to Spain. On the 1st of November, 1768, De Ulloa and his family repaired to a French vessel which he had chartered, and amid the derisive shouts of the people and their patriotic songs he sailed away from the town of New Orleans. The French governor was compelled to order back a force of the French colonists who persisted in following as far as the French fort at the Balize, there to oppose any Spanish aid entering the river.

Upon Aubry's threat to fire upon the insurgents following De Ulloa's ship, they desisted, and in his report to the French government detailing this circumstance, he says: "On that occasion I was obeyed for the first time."

The people attempted to vindicate their expulsion of De Ulloa with various pretexts detrimental to his administration, but the real motive is too plainly revealed in the concluding part of their attempted justification, where they say: "What harm have we done in shaking off a foreign yoke which was made still more heavy and crushing by the hand which imposed it? What offense have we committed in claiming back our laws, our country, our sovereign, and in consecrating to him our everlasting love?" They appealed to the King to annul the cession and to restore to them French sovereignty.

The weakness of France which prompted the cession to Spain still remained, however, to forbid a recession.

The Spanish ministry took up the sedition in Louisiana. But one minister advised the King in favor of receding the province to France. The council, with this exception, while admitting the antipathy of the colonists to Spanish rule, and the vast expense of maintaining local government with no corresponding revenue to follow, held that for State policies it were best to retain the cession. The Mississippi River formed a line of demarcation between the Spanish and the

English possessions. Between Louisiana and Mexico there intervened a vast space within which another power might encroach by extending its frontier, and thus produce incessant controversy with Spain, while with France in control of Louisiana, that power might in time extend itself toward Mexico and open up an illicit trade with that country, as was previously done; and further, in the event the English should prevail over the French, it might be to the interest of France, in the settlement of terms, to offer Louisiana to the English nation, which would be unfortunate for Spain as respects her Spanish possessions adjacent. It was therefore determined to retain the cession, and while reorganizing the local government upon a Spanish foundation it was proposed to visit punishment upon the leaders of the late insurrection. The King himself expressed a firm resolution to recover possession and to repress all designs against his authority in the province.

The determination of the government was made painfully manifest to the colonists when, on July 24, 1769, there appeared before New Orleans a formidable Spanish fleet of 24 sail and a force of 2,600 men, under the command of General O'Reilly, a famous commander, who had been selected to receive formal possession of Louisiana and defend the Spanish possession. The first act after the formal cession was the arrest and trial of the leaders of the late revolution. They were found guilty and some cruelly condemned to death, some were sentenced to perpetual imprisonment and others to lesser punishment, while as to all confiscation of property was adjudged.

SPAIN CEDES FLORIDA TO GREAT BRITAIN.

By another section of the treaty of 1763, Havana and the whole of Cuba, which then belonged to Great Britain, were restored to Spain, and in return therefor Spain ceded to Great Britain "Florida, with Fort St. Augustin and the bay of Pensacola, as well as all that Spain possesses on the continent of North America to the east or to the southeast of the river Mississippi."

If it were true that the cession to Spain of "the country known under the name of Louisiana," contained West Florida, or any portion east of the Mississippi which might be said to conflict with the later grant from France to Great Britain, this was corrected in the cession by Spain to Great Britain of "all that Spain possesses on the continent of North America to the east of or to the southeast of the river Mississippi."

To this point we find England claiming possession of all that France possessed to the east or southeast of the Mississippi and, also, all that Spain possessed and claimed eastward of that river. Spain retained possession of her recent cession from France of the territory situated west of the Mississippi, with the city and island of New Orleans. Great Britain now became possessed of the Florida territory, whatever that was, of the French territory on the river and port of Mobile and all that remained of the original Louisiana of La Salle's claim east of the Mississippi. This rounded out England's posesssions. The Atlantic was the eastern boundary, the Mississippi the western, and the Gulf the southeast, with her Canadian possessions on the north. It will be noticed how possession followed according to the law of discovery. The Spaniards claimed Florida through the Tampa, Pensacola and St. Augustine settlements and discoveries; and France claimed the country drained by the river and bay of Mobile, and the greater country drained by the Mississippi, on like grounds.

Much confusion exists in the popular mind as to the treaties between the Great Powers in 1762 and 1763. First in order was the single and complete cession of "the whole country known by the name of Louisiana," by and on the part of the King of France to the King of Spain. This was November 3, 1762, and is known in history as the "Family Compact," and so known because of the agreement between the two monarchs that they would defend each other in their dominions throughout the world, and would regard as a common enemy any nation which should antagonize either. Second in order was the treaty—about three months later—between the Kings of Great Britain, Portugal, Spain and France, which was concluded February 10, 1763, known as the Treaty of Paris and in which the King of France cedes "everything of which he possesses on the left side of the river Mississippi" to Great Britain. Since, in all the claims of France previously made, the country of Louisiana was understood to embrace territory on the left side of the Mississippi, as well as on the right side, as shown in the grant to Antoine de Crozat, September 14, 1712, by Louis XIV, which was "bounded by the English Carolinas" and designated as a part of "the country of Louisiana," and so described on the early French maps and by French explorers and French writers, it naturally excites surprise that in the face of the cession to Spain of the "whole country known as Louisiana," there should also be ceded a part of that same Louisiana to Great Britain a few months later. It may be said that the treaty of November 3, 1762, was well named the "Secret Treaty." The surprise is the greater when it is known that the preliminaries of this second treaty were actually signed on the same day as that ceding "all of Louisiana to Spain."

TALLEYRAND'S EXPLANATION.

That we may also have before us the justification of France and Spain for such evident inconsistency, if not deception, it may be of interest to read the letter from Talleyrand to General Armstrong after the cession, and thus we have both sides of the controversy fairly presented, and for this purpose the letter follows:

[American State Papers (foreign relations), vol. 2, p. 635. Letter from M. Talleyrand to General Armstrong.

PARIS, *December 21, 1804.*

SIR: I had the honor, in Brumaire last, to inform Mr. Livingston that I would submit to the inspection of His Imperial Majesty the letters he addressed to me relative to the motives of Mr. Monroe's journey to Spain, and some discussions between the Court of Madrid and the United States.

Among the observations made on this subject by Messrs. Livingston and Monroe, His Imperial Majesty has been obliged to give particular attention to those bearing on the discussions, of which the object is peculiarly interesting to the French Government. He has perceived that he could not have been a stranger to the examination of these discussions since they grew out of the treaty by which France had ceded Louisiana to the United States; and His Majesty has thought that an explanation, made with that fidelity which characterizes him, on the eastern boundaries of the ceded territory, would put an end to the differences to which this cession has given rise.

France in giving up Louisiana to the United States, transferred to them all the rights over that colony which she had acquired from Spain; she could not, nor did she wish to, cede any other; and, that no room might be left for doubt in this respect she repeated, in her treaty of 30th April, 1803, the literal expressions of the treaty of St. Ildefonso, by which she had acquired that colony two years before.

Now it was stipulated, in her treaty of the year 1801, that the acquisition of Louisiana by France was a *retrocession;* that is to say, that Spain restored to France what she has received from her in 1762. At that period she had received the territory bounded on east by the Mississippi, the river Iberville and the lakes Maurepas and Pontchartrain; the same day France ceded to England, by the preliminaries of peace, all the territory to the eastward. Of this Spain had received no part, and could, therefore give back none to France.

All the territory lying to the eastward of the Mississippi and the river Iberville, and south of the 32d degree of north latitude, bears the name of Florida. It has been constantly designated in that way during the time that Spain held it; it bears the same name in the treaties of limits between Spain and the United States; and, in different notes of Mr. Livingston of a later date than the treaty of retrocession, in which the name of Louisiana is given to the territory on the west side of the Mississippi; of Florida to that on the east of it.

According to this designation, thus consecrated by time, and even prior to the period when Spain began to possess the whole territory between the 31st degree, the Mississippi, and the sea, this country ought, in good faith and justice, to be distinguished from Louisiana.

Your excellency knows that before the preliminaries of 1762, confirmed by the treaty of 1763, the French possessions, situated near the Mississippi, extended as far from the east of this river, towards the Ohio and the Illinois, as in the quarters of Mobile; and you must think it as unnatural, after all the changes of sovereignty which that part of America has undergone, to give the name of Louisiana to the district of Mobile, as to the territory more to the north, on the same bank of the river, which formerly belonged to France.

These observations, sir, will be sufficient to dispel every kind of doubt, with regard to the extent of the retrocession made by Spain to France, in the month of Vendemiaire, year 9. It was under this impression that the French and Spanish plenipotentiaries negotiated, and it was under this impression that I have since had occasion to give the necessary explanations when a project was formed to take possession of it. I have laid before His Imperial Majesty the negotiations of Madrid which preceded the treaty of 1801, and His Majesty is convinced that, during the whole course of these negotiations, the Spanish Government has constantly refused to cede any part of the Floridas, even from the Mississippi to Mobile.

His Imperial Majesty has, moreover, authorized me to declare to you, that, at the beginning of the year 11, General Bournonville was charged to open a new negotiation with Spain for the acquisition of the Floridas. This project, which has not been followed by any treaty, is an evident proof that France had not acquired, by the treaty retroceding Louisiana, the country east of the Mississippi.

The candor of these observations proves to you, sir, how much value His Majesty attaches to the maintenance of a good understanding between two Powers, to whom France is united by connexions so intimate and so numerous. His Majesty called upon to give explanations on a question which interested France directly, persuades himself that they will leave no ground of misunderstanding between the United States and Spain; and that these two Powers, animated, as they ought to be, by sentiments of friendship which their vicinity and their position render so necessary, will be able to agree with the same facility on the other subjects of their discussion.

This result His Imperial Majesty will learn with real interest. He saw with pain the United States commence their differences with Spain in an unusual manner, and conduct themselves towards the Floridas by acts of violence which not being founded in right, could have no other effect but to injure its lawful owners. * * *

[*This letter not quoted in full.*]

THE FLORIDAS RETROCEDED TO SPAIN.

Twenty years later (on September 3, 1783) another treaty was consummated in which Great Britain and Spain were again contracting parties, wherein Great Britain, in consideration for an exchange of the Bahama Islands, owned by Spain, re-ceded to that nation East and West Florida; and thus for the second time Spain became possessed of Florida. Further on it will be important to remember that in all the cessions and retrocessions between the different claimants to the Mississippi country, Spain acquired from France no interest to any country east of the Mississippi and the island and city of New Orleans. What Spain acquired in that quarter was from a different source entirely. It is also well to remember that France had disposed of all her possessions on both sides of the river. She conveyed to Spain "all the country known under the name of Louisiana, as well as New Orleans and the island on which that place stands," and conveyed to Britain all her possessions "on the left side of the river Mississippi," except the island and city of New Orleans. If Great Britain held any portion of Louisiana under the cession from Spain of West Florida (and, under Spain's claim, such portion may have been included), then, by the retrocession, Spain became repossessed of so much of *the* Louisiana which France had possessed.

THE UNITED STATES AND SPAIN.

The war of our revolution coming on, and the colonies having succeeded against Great Britain, the United States now appear in history as a nation, to contest with her neighbors for adjustment of boundary lines which before were undetermined, and on October 27, 1795, a treaty was entered into between our nation and Spain in which it was agreed that "the southern boundary of the United States, which divides their territory from the Spanish colonies of East and West Florida, shall be designated by a line beginning on the river Mississippi at the northernmost part of the thirty-first degree of latitude north of the equator, which from thence shall be drawn due east to the middle of the river Apalachicola or Catahouchie; thence along the middle thereof to its junction with the Flint; thence straight to the head of St. Marys river, and thence down the middle thereof to the Atlantic Ocean."

While this settled how far north Spain might extend her Florida boundary, no occasion then existed for determining the western boundary, as Spain owned on both sides of the Mississippi. What was claimed as West Florida became a source of trouble later on. Spain and the United States were now the only neighbors.

AMERICAN SETTLEMENTS.

The navigation of the Mississippi.— By gradual advances the course of American empire at last spread as far westward as the valley of the Mississippi; and by various treaties with foreign nations and with Indian tribes, the supremacy of the infant republic had already reach d the "father of waters." Beyond was Spanish territory. The mouth of that great river was under foreign control. Spain possessed both banks at that point. Our line of settlements depended upon that river as a highway to the markets. Their products must pass out through the mouth of the Mississippi. The free navigation of this river was therefore a matter of vital concern. There was but one interest, one demand, one hope and one expression on the part of every American in that portion of the extended empire, and that was for the free right of way over these waters from the head of navigation to the sea. That spirit of resistance to intervening obstacles, coupled with love of right and freedom which characterized the builders of our nation, and which went with the advance immigration into the forest wilds and upon the desert plains, asserted itself in the valley of the Mississippi and demanded a free outlet. Whenever this right had been granted it was only of a temporary nature, and even then permitted with reluctance and under restriction. When, therefore, it was rumored that Spain had ceded Louisiana to France, fears were at once aroused lest the French should exercise even a more exclusive and vigorous policy than had the Spaniards, from whom, by the treaty of October 27, 1795, a right was secured to deposit the merchandise and effects of the Americans at New Orleans for the space of three years, and at the end of that period the agreement stipulated that "the privilege should either be continued at New Orleans or an equivalent establishment assigned on another part of the banks of the Mississippi." Even after the lapse of the three years a tacit permission continued. The Spaniards declined to believe the reported cession of the province to France, but resolved if it were true not to relinquish their authority without protest.

Following this came the announcement that the Spanish intendant had proclaimed that the right of deposit no longer existed. This produced an outburst of intense indignation from the Americans, and remonstrance came from the settlers and planters on lands tributary to the Mississippi. It was at once assumed that the Spanish revocation was a result of the cession to France, and, further, that it was secretly prompted in advance by the latter power. This naturally made the cession to France the more obnoxious. Angry and excited appeals and urgent petitions were addressed to Congress. The conclusion was everywhere irresistible that a policy of exclusion was to be the order which would mean the extinction of American commerce and navigation rights along the Mississippi and the abandonment of flourishing communities already established there. That feeling so inherent in the American breast of resistance to arbitrary power began to assert itself. "The Mississippi is ours by the law of nature," the inhabitants proclaimed. Proceeding still further they threatened in their remonstrance: "If Congress refuses us effectual protection, if it forsakes us, we will adopt the measures which our safety requires, even if they endanger the peace of the Union and our connection with the other States. No protection, no allegiance."

POPULAR DISCONTENT.

The people in the older States along the Atlantic seaboard caught up the cry from their relatives and fellow-countrymen on the then distant frontiers of Ohio, Kentucky, Tennessee and Indiana, and emphasized the demand on Congress and on the President for relief through negotiation, or, if that failed, by war. It became a party issue. President Jefferson foresaw the growing discontent, and endeavored to allay the excitement by assurance of every possible effort on his part as the nation's Executive. He transmitted to Congress, December 22, 1802, a message in which he said "that he was aware of the obligation to maintain in all cases the rights of the nation, and to employ for that purpose those just and honorable means which belong to the character of the United States." In a reply from the House of Representatives, that body reminded the President that they held it to be their duty "to express their unalterable determination to maintain the boundaries and the rights of navigation and commerce through the river Mississippi as established by existing treaties."

ATTEMPTS TO SECURE COMMERCIAL PRIVILEGES.

The President in the meanwhile had been active. Through Charles Pinckney, the minister of the United States to Madrid, he offered to purchase of Spain that nation's possessions on the east side of the Mississippi, and as a further inducement, and in the event of purchase, the United States offered to guarantee the Spanish dominions beyond the Mississippi. Jefferson instructed Pinckney to say to the Spanish monarch:

> The anxiety of our Government on the subject of possessing the territory on the east side of the Mississippi, the importance of this acquisition to them for the purpose of securing to the citizens of one-half of the United States the certain means of exporting their products, " feel themselves every day more convinced of their having a permanent establishment on the Mississippi, convenient for the purposes of navigation, and belonging solely to them.

The Spanish Government declined this offer, and even refused the further request that a mercantile agent of the United States be permitted to reside at New Orleans, the answer being: "That by making one example of that kind the door would be opened for like demands on the part of other nations." This refusal was dated April 7, 1802, more than one year and a half after the secret treaty ceding Louisiana with New Orleans to France (October 1, 1800). Though Mr. Pinckney was at the court of Spain, and diplomatic correspondence had passed between him and that court as to our anxiety concerning the free navigation of the Mississippi, yet the cession to France was not even hinted to him, and he, as well as Mr. Jefferson, still supposed Spain to own both sides of that river at its mouth.

SPAIN RETROCEDES TO FRANCE.

The next important change in the relations of Louisiana was in the retrocession from Spain to France in the treaty known as the "treaty of San Ildefonso," October 1, 1800. Spain had held possession for thirty-eight years. The Duke of Parma, a son-in-law of the King of Spain, was desirous of securing for himself the succession to the Grand Duchy of Tuscany, that he should be raised to the dignity of a king and have his dominions enlarged by the addition of Tuscany. In consideration of France giving assurances for these distinctions and enlarged territory in Italy, Spain agreed to cede Louisiana.

The action of Spain was as great a surprise as it was a disappointment to the people of the United States. Jefferson voiced the popular sentiment when, on December 15, 1802, he said to Congress: "The cession of the Spanish province of Louisiana to France, which took place in the course of the late war, will, if carried into effect, make a change in the aspect of our foreign relations." Our recent communications with France had not been of a pleasant character.

Our shipping upon the high seas had for some time been exposed to unexpected depredations by French cruisers. Protest after protest had been made to the French government, and various offers for amicable terms proposed, but without avail. Washington had frequent occasion to complain, and this condition continued into the administration of President John Adams, who sent an embassy to France in 1798 to adjust the differences between the two nations. The French Directory added insult to injury by refusing to give audience to the embassy. Assurances were finally given that upon payment of a liberal sum to the French government and a gratuity of a quarter of a million dollars to Talleyrand—who was one of the Directory—the Americans would be heard. It was in reply to this shameful demand that Charles Cotesworth Pinckney, one of the embassy, made that memorable answer: "Millions for defense, but not one cent for tribute," and with his colleagues, John Marshall and Elbridge Gerry, returned to their own country. This outrage was met by Adams in preparations for war, and Washington, then in retirement at Mount Vernon, was requested by the President to take command of our armies. He accepted, and chose his friend Alexander Hamilton as his second in command. The promptness and determination of our nation to resent the long-suffered abuses upon our commerce and the personal indignities offered our accredited diplomatic representatives, aroused the French to a realization that we would give them war, unless they should give us fair dealing. They chose the latter alternative and terms were agreed upon, but not until the accession to power of the astute First Consul, who clearly foresaw the complications which his predecessors in authority had invited as to us and as to other nations with which France was destined to engage in very costly and unprofitable wars.

This episode in the dismissal of Pinckney, Marshall and Gerry, our three special envoys, which led to the suspension of our commercial intercourse with France, when added to the well-known reputation of Napoleon for aggressive demands among those who were his neighbors, made any closer relations at that time with him or his nation exceedingly distasteful. Mr. Jefferson preferred that Spain should be our neighbor rather than France.

The specific words of the retrocession are as follows:

> His Catholic Majesty promises and engages on his part to retrocede to the French Republic * * * the colony or province of Louisiana with the same extent it now has in the hands of Spain, and that it had when France possessed it, and such as it should be after the treaty subsequently entered into between Spain and other States.

The actual existence of the retrocession now being known it only increased the previous ill feeling occasioned by the mere rumor. The exact text of the treaty of Ildefonso, however, was unknown until published in the Memoir by De Onis in 1820. To what extent did France recover possession of Louisiana as it formerly belonged to her? This was the question.

To still more complicate the situation, war between France and England was about to become an assured fact. It was therefore determined at once to press negotiations upon France for terms. The exigency seemed to require the best effort and the best talent, and, to that end, James Monroe was selected to cooperate with Mr. Livingston, our minister to Napoleon's court. In addition to Mr. Monroe's high qualifications he was specially recommended because of his previous attitude, while a Member of Congress from Virginia, in asserting the rights of the western people to the navigation of their great river. It became very evident to Mr. Jefferson that unless a favorable result was secured through negotiation a resort must be had to war, and he even went so far as to instruct our ministers to consult with England with a view to an alliance against France. His language to Minister Livingston is significant:

> The day that France takes possession of New Orleans fixes the sentence which is to restrain her forever within her low-water mark. It seals the union of two nations who in conjunction can maintain exclusive possession of the ocean. From that moment we must marry ourselves to the British fleet and nation. * * * This is not a state we seek or desire. It is one which this measure, if adopted by France, forces on us as necessarily as any other cause, by the laws of nature, brings on its necessary effect.

The anxiety and deep feeling which possessed Mr. Jefferson can be seen in the hurried note which he addressed to Mr. Monroe:

> I have but a moment to inform you that the fever into which the western mind is thrown by the affair at New Orleans, stimulated by the mercantile and generally the federal interest, threatens to overbear our peace. * * *
> I shall to-morrow nominate you to the Senate for an extraordinary mission to France. * * * In the meantime pray work night and day to arrange your affairs for a temporary absence, perhaps for a long one. * * *

A few days later he again wrote him, saying:

> The agitation of the public mind on occasion of the late suspension of our rights of deposit at New Orleans is extreme. * * * Remonstrances, memorials, etc., are now circulating through the whole of the country, and signing by the body of the people. The measures which we have been pursuing, being invisible, do not satisfy their minds; something sensible, therefore, has become necessary, and, indeed, our object of purchasing New Orleans and the Floridas is a measure likely to assume so many shapes that no instructions could be squared to fit them.

THE LOUISIANA PURCHASE.

NEW ORLEANS AND FLORIDA ARE DEMANDED.

Here we observe the first distinct demand on the part of our people. To have asked more would have been extremely unpopular at that time. Napoleon, who was now confronted with the certainty of a gigantic war with England, well knew that colonies far distant across the seas must be protected by sufficient naval forces and at great cost. England was then a great naval power while France was far inferior. The recent French losses in San Domingo, with the proximity to Louisiana of the British naval armaments in that quarter, with well-equipped garrisons in Jamaica and the Windward Islands, required but little reflection for an astute mind like that of Napoleon to suggest the most disastrous consequences if immediate action by him should not be adopted as to Louisiana. He was not long in arriving at a conclusion. Summoning two of his counsellors to him, and in a very impassioned manner, he disclosed to them his purpose with regard to Louisiana. He said :

> They (the English) shall not have the Mississippi, which they covet. * * * The conquest of Louisiana would be easy if they only took the trouble to make a descent there. I have not a moment to lose in putting it out of their reach. * * * I think of ceding it to the United States. * * * They only ask of me one town in Louisiana, but I already consider the colony as entirely lost ; and it appears to me that in the hands of this growing power it will be more useful to the policy, and even to the commerce, of France, than if I should attempt to keep it.

NAPOLEON OFFERS TO CEDE ALL OF LOUISIANA.

The two counsellors disagreed, one approving the course proposed and the other decidedly opposing it. To the first one Napoleon communicated his final resolution, saying :

> It is not only New Orleans that I will cede, it is the whole colony without any reservation. * * * To attempt to retain it would be folly. I direct you to negotiate this offer with the envoys of the United States. * * * I will be moderate in consideration of the necessity in which I am of making a sale. But keep this to yourself.

It was Napoleon's belief that Monroe was clothed with instructions more extensive than the assumed authorization of Congress would warrant, both as to territory and as to price. In this he was mistaken. The instructions to our envoys were to "procure * * * a cession to the United States of New Orleans and of West and East Florida, or as much thereof as the actual proprietor can be prevailed on to part with."

It was also required that "the navigation of the river Mississippi, in its whole breadth from its source to the ocean and in all its passages to and from the same, shall be equally free and common to citizens of the United States and of the French Republic." It was suggested that if France declined to cede to us the whole of the island of Orleans then a part should be sought for, if no more than space enough upon which to establish a large commercial town on the bank of the river; or if unable to procure a complete jurisdiction over any convenient spot

THOMAS JEFFERSON, 1743, AT AGE OF 70

Barbé Marbois.

whatever, the envoys were instructed to secure a right of deposit with the privilege of holding real estate for commercial purposes. If the Floridas could not be secured the envoys were to seek for suitable deposits at the mouths of the rivers passing from the United States through the Floridas, as well as their free navigation.

TWO PROMINENT ACTORS.

There are two eminent persons in history to whose utterances at this distant day we can refer with confidence for authoritative information as to the details of the negotiations for, and as to what was included in, the Louisiana cession, and these are Marbois and Jefferson—the one of France, the other of America; the one, who was Napoleon's negotiator, in selling; the other, who was our President, in buying Louisiana. These men, as the noted representatives of the two countries in this transaction, may well be depended on to convey to us the most accurate information touching the cession in all its phases.

Marquis de Marbois had a most intimate personal knowledge of our country and had contributed valuable aid in our revolutionary struggle. He was also a diplomat of wide experience, having served in 1769 as secretary of the French legation to the diet of the Empire, which held its sittings at Ratisbon; later he served in the same character at Dresden, and was chargé d'affaires at Bavaria, and was afterwards elected counsellor of the parliament of Metz. In 1779 he was made secretary of the French legation and while here married an American, a resident of Philadelphia; at all times he was a most devoted friend of our Republic. On his return to France his active temperament soon brought him in contact with the varying changes of government at that time. He suffered imprisonment, ostracism, and exile at some periods, while at others he enjoyed the most distinguished honors. During the reign of terror he was imprisoned, and recovered his liberty only with the fall of Robespierre. When Napoleon became First Consul he treated Marbois with marked favor, and in 1801 made him minister of the public treasury. During the negotiations for the cession of the Louisiana territory he was selected by Napoleon as plenipotentiary on the part of the French Republic. So grave a matter should properly have been intrusted to Talleyrand, but Mr. Monroe, in his memoirs tells us that Napoleon, addressing Marbois, said, "That being an affair of the treasury, I will commit it to you." It is, however, asserted that this was not the real motive for intrusting this negotiation to Marbois, but was done because Napoleon had greater confidence in his integrity than he had in Talleyrand's.

The following extract from a letter from Livingston to Madison, of April 13, 1803, may here be of interest, as it refers to M. Marbois, who related to Livingston an interview that he had with the First Consul:

> He (Marbois) then took occasion to mention his sorrow that any cause of difference should exist between our countries. The Consul told him, in reply, "Well, you have the charge of the treasury; let them give you one hundred million of Francs, and pay their own claims, and take the whole country." Seeing by my looks that I was surprised at so extravagant a demand, he added that he considered the demand as exorbitant, and had told the First Consul that the thing was impossible; that

we had not the means of raising that. The Consul [asked] him we might borrow it. I now plainly saw the whole business: first, the Consul was disposed [to se]ll; next, he distrusted Talleyrand, on account of the business of the supposed intention to bri[be, a]nd meant to put the negotiation into the hands of Marbois, whose character for integrity is established. (See American State Papers, Foreign Relations, vol. 2, p. 553.)

Whether this be true or otherwise, it is certain that our negotiators had great admiration for Marbois, as Monroe, in referring to the success obtained, says:

I add with pleasure that the conduct of M. Marbois, in every stage of the negotiations, was liberal, candid and fair, indicating a very friendly feeling for the United States and a strong desire to preserve the most amicable relations between the two countries.

THE AMERICAN NEGOTIATORS.

At this time Robert R. Livingston was the American minister to Paris. He had been judge of the admiralty court, a justice of the New York supreme court, and a member of the stamp act Congress in 1765. He was a delegate to the Continental Congress, where he was chosen one of a committee of five to draft the Declaration of Independence. He was appointed the first chancellor of New York and as such administered the oath of office to George Washington on his inauguration as first President of the United States. He was Secretary of Foreign Affairs for the United States from 1781 to 1783. In 1801 he resigned the chancellorship and accepted the mission to France.

James Monroe, as before mentioned, was also appointed to aid in the negotiations, and was named as minister extraordinary. His life had been an eventful one. He joined the army in the revolution at the headquarters of Washington in New York as a lieutenant; was with the troops at Harlem, White Plains and Trenton; he also took part in the battles of Brandywine, Germantown and Monmouth. He was a Representative in the Fourth, Fifth and Sixth Congresses of the Confederation; was elected a United States Senator from Virginia in 1790, and held the office for four years, when he was sent as envoy to France. He was governor of Virginia from 1799 to 1802. After Jefferson's election to the Presidency he was returned to the French mission from which a few years before he had been recalled. From Paris he went to London as the accredited representative of the United States to the Court of St. James. After his return he was chosen for the second time governor of Virginia, and afterwards became Secretary of State under President Madison. In 1814-15 he acted as Secretary of War. In 1816, at the age of 59, he was elected President of the United States, and was reelected in 1821 with almost complete unanimity. Under his administration much important legislation was enacted; he became conspicuous in his resistance to foreign interference in American affairs, and his name has become associated with the policy ever since known as the Monroe Doctrine, which now has the force of international law. His appointment to Paris at this particular time was a very popular one, especially in view of the well-known record he had made in advocacy of the American claim to the free navigation of the Mississippi

Robert R. Livingston.

PRESIDENT MONROE.

river. Much was expected of him, and well this confidence was rep... as the result testified. His splendid service in the achievement accomplished was in after years remembered, when he was elected to the Chief Magistracy of the nation.

These were the eminent Americans who were to arrange the terms of purchase with the French negotiator. All had been intimate before and had contributed mutual aid in the establishment of our Republic. Livingston, Monroe and Marbois now met on the shores of another nation as envoys of two different countries, and though friends were yet loyal to the conflicting interests and to the opposite sovereignties which they respectively represented.

So great an acquisition as the Louisiana territory was never contemplated when these envoys entered upon their duties. Such thoughts were never entertained by Jefferson, Madison, Monroe or Livingston. It was nowhere discussed in our nation. For the Floridas and for New Orleans our envoys were authorized to offer $2,000,000. Jefferson feared to the last moment that even the least of his proposals would be rejected by France. While Livingston, the American minister at Paris, was exceedingly nervous and never confident; various efforts were made by him before Monroe's arrival to reach some terms. When Talleyrand met Livingston, after the stormy interview between himself, Napoleon and Marbois, he astounded him when he very abruptly inquired, "What will you give for the whole?" So unexpected was this, it was difficult for him to make reply. The following day he summoned courage to follow up this advantage; approaching Talleyrand on the proposition for the cession of the whole of Louisiana, Talleyrand explained that the suggestion was only personal from himself. Livingston, writing to Madison at the time of this interview, says: "He (Talleyrand) told me he would answer my note, but that he must do it evasively, because Louisiana was not theirs." This only made Livingston thereafter the more suspicious and led him strongly to believe that the delays were intended only to gain time. Even when Marbois seriously submitted to him a like proposition he hesitated to confide in his good faith. He also realized that he was without authority to entertain such an enlarged scheme, however sincerely offered. While the true condition remained unknown to him, and while he was still suffering the greatest distrust of his surroundings, Monroe arrived; at his first meeting with his colleague, Livingston said to him, "Only force can give us New Orleans. We must employ force. Let us first get possession of the country and negotiate afterwards." A conference on the following day with Marbois soon convinced Monroe of the victory which was close at hand. Marbois, being delighted to meet his old friend of the revolutionary days, frankly confided to him the conclusion of Napoleon with a reliable statement of the motives for the same. The overtures by Marbois were received with surprise and delight. It was impossible to realize the magnitude of the prize. As Marbois in after years so well says in his writings:

Instead of the cession of a town and its inconsiderable territory a vast portion of America was in some sort offered to the United States. They only asked for the mere right of navigating the Mississippi, and their sovereignty was about to be extended over the largest rivers of the world.

LOUISIANA CEDED TO THE UNITED STATES.

The American envoys could not consult the home government for further instructions. The distance was great and time was precious. War was soon to be declared between England and France. Prompt action was necessary. Quickness in action meant the vast domain west of the Mississippi for our Republic, as delay in action would mean it for England. Our negotiators read the future with the alternative before them, and they gladly accepted the issue, and soon there was an agreement for the cession of the whole of Louisiana. It was Marbois who submitted the draft which contained this clause:

> The colony or province of Louisiana is ceded by France to the United States, with all its rights and appurtenances, as fully and in the same manner as they have been acquired by the French Republic, by virtue of the third article of the treaty concluded with His Catholic Majesty at St. Ildephonso on the 1st of October, 1800.

This language was subsequently changed and when made a part of the final treaty the clause was as follows:

> ART. 1. Whereas by the article the third of the treaty concluded at St. Ildefonso, the 9th Vendémiaire, an. 9 (1st October, 1800,) between the First Consul of the French Republic and his catholic majesty, it was agreed as follows: "His catholic majesty promises and engages on his part, to cede to the French Republic, six months after the full and entire execution of the conditions and stipulations herein relative to his royal highness, the Duke of Parma, the colony or province of Louisiana, with the same extent that it now has in the hands of Spain, and that it had when France possessed it, and such as it should be after the treaties subsequently entered into between Spain and other States." And whereas, in pursuance of the treaty, and particularly of the third article, the French Republic has an incontestible title to the domain and to the possession of the said territory: The First Consul of the French Republic desiring to give to the United States a strong proof of his friendship, doth hereby cede to the said United States, in the name of the French Republic, forever and in full sovereignty, the said territory, with all its rights and appurtenances, as fully and in the same manner as they have been acquired by the French Republic, in virtue of the above-mentioned treaty, concluded with His catholic majesty.

Did France recover possession of the Louisiana it formerly owned and, if so, was not that Louisiana the same as now ceded to the United States? This was a vital question.

INDEFINITE BOUNDARIES.

As this description was very vague and unsatisfactory as to the definite boundaries and extent of the purchase, our envoys quite properly insisted upon a more specific identification. The domain to the east of the Mississippi had all been determined by various treaties, and the claims of the different nations were generally well known, though some were not conceded; yet the great empire lying to the west of the Mississippi continued to remain a source of much trouble and uncertainty, as no satisfactory data were offered for specific boundary, and none could be agreed upon. Marbois expressed to Napoleon the difficulty in reaching a definite conclusion as to boundary, and regretted the obscurity in which so important a reference was made, but this did not trouble the conscience of Napoleon, who replied, "that if an obscurity did not already exist, it would, perhaps, be good policy to put one there." Even when questioned as to the eastern boundary, evasive answers were returned. Livingston asked Talleyrand for the description contained in the instructions given by his nation previously to Laussat, and which contained a definition of the cession. "What are the eastern bounds of Louisiana?" asked Livingston. "I do not know," replied Talleyrand. "You must take it as we received it." "But what did you mean to take?" said Livingston. "I do not know," replied Talleyrand. "Then you mean that we shall construe it our own way?" said Livingston again, to which Talleyrand made final reply, "I can give you no direction. You have made a noble bargain for yourselves, and I suppose you will make the most of it."

Our envoys did not worry long over this vexed problem. They were as eager as the French to close the bargain and take the chances and, if need be, rely on future treaty stipulations for more certainty as to boundaries. It is evident that careful attention was not given to the agreement as an entirety, as many omissions were subsequently observed, which, if more care had been taken in its preparation would never have occurred, but as Livingston wrote to Madison: "I was willing to take it under any form." The price agreed upon was finally fixed at 60,000,000 francs, in the form of United States 6 per cent bonds, in value $11,250,000; and in addition to this our Government assumed the payment of certain debts due to our own citizens valued at 20,000,000 francs, or $3,750,000, making as the total consideration paid, $15,000,000. When we consider that Jefferson at one time was willing to give $2,000,000 for New Orleans alone, we can well marvel that so vast an empire as the whole province should come to us for the price paid. We can afford to overlook any defects in the treaty details, and forever hold in gratitude the illustrious men who, by their diplomatic skill, their earnestness of purpose, and well-directed efforts, achieved one of the greatest triumphs in the world's history, and which, one historian writes, "ranked in historical importance next to the Declaration of Independence and the adoption of the Constitution."

It well justified the boast of Livingston as he placed his name to the treaty of cession, and rising and shaking hands with Monroe and Marbois, said: "We have lived long, but this is the noblest work of our lives."

RATIFICATIONS EXCHANGED.

The treaties were sent to Washington as fast as possible, as it was Napoleon's desire that ratifications should be exchanged at Washington rather than at Paris. By this course he hoped to gain time on England, as this assured him an earlier payment of the money for the purchase. The papers arrived at Washington July 14, 1803, and October 17, following, Congress was convened; after much discussion and contention as to the constitutional authority of Congress to annex foreign territory to the Union, the treaty was ratified. Even with all this done our anxieties were not at an end, nor our purchase secure. Up to this moment,

Louisiana still remained in the possession and under the government of Spain. There had as yet been no surrender to France under the treaty of St. Ildefonso, October 1, 1800, and three years had elapsed since then. France was not in the occupancy of the purchase to comply with the treaty negotiated with the Americans. Indeed, when at last the treaty was made known to the Spaniards in Louisiana and even in Spain, protests were received at Washington from both quarters. The Spanish minister served notice on our Government—

that he had orders to warn the Federal Government to suspend the ratification and execution of the treaties of cession of Louisiana, as the French Government in securing the province had contracted an engagement with Spain not to retrocede it to any other power, * * * France not having executed that engagement, the treaty cession was void.

It was thought by many that England had united with Spain to defeat the purchase. The French Government had given orders that both transfers of authority should take place at New Orleans at the same time, so as to expedite the surrender to the United States before England could intervene.

POSSESSION TAKEN.

Regardless of the Spanish protests, the French chargé d'affaires at Washington transmitted instructions to the representative of his government at New Orleans for the transfer. The messenger reached there on the 23d of November, 1803. A conference followed between the French and Spanish officials and it was agreed to make the change. The Spanish troops and militia were arrayed in solemn procession, and in presence of those assembled the commissioners representing France and Spain proclaimed the missions they were charged to execute. The French commissioner presented to the Spanish commissioner the order of the King of Spain for the delivery of the province, dated more than one year previous, and with this was also presented the direction of Napoleon to receive possession in the name of France. The Spanish governor then surrendered the keys of the city, and thereupon the authority of Spain was withdrawn and the Spanish colors lowered, as the banners of France were unfurled to the breeze amid the booming of artillery. The authority of France continued for the brief period of twenty days, and then the last change was to occur, when the Stars and Stripes were to wave over the great empire west of the Mississippi and over the island of New Orleans. On December 20, 1803, the American troops marched into the metropolis and the French prefect sadly announced:

In conformity with the treaty I put the United States in possession of Louisiana and its dependencies. The citizens and inhabitants who wish to remain here and obey the laws are from this moment exonerated from the oath of fidelity to the French Republic.

Thereupon the American governor, with patriotic delight, addressing the concourse present, said:

The cession secures to you and your descendants the inheritance of liberty, perpetual laws, and magistrates whom you will elect yourselves.

As the French colors came down and the Red, White and Blue of the American Republic went up, the trumpets sounded, the troops saluted, and gladsome voices shouted long and loud in honor of one of the greatest events in our history.

A RIVALRY FOR HONOR.

As every authentic reference to the history of this cession is of precious value at this day, I can not refrain from adding an extract from one of Mr. Livingston's letters, tending to show the zealous pride he felt for his participation in that success, and his desire that the credit for the negotiation should be given to him rather than to Mr. Monroe:

> I have in my former letter informed you of M. Talleyrand's calling upon me previous to the arrival of Mr. Monroe, for a proposition for the whole of Louisiana; of his afterwards trifling with me, and telling me *that what he said was unauthorized*. This circumstance, for which I have accounted to you in one of my letters, led me to think, though it afterwards appeared without reason, that some change had taken place in the determination which I knew the Consul had before taken to sell. I had just then received a line from Mr. Monroe, informing me of his arrival. I wrote a hasty answer, under the influence of ideas, excited by these prevarications of the minister, expressing the hope that he had brought information that New Orleans was in our possession; that I hoped our negotiations might be successful; but that, while I feared nothing but war would avail us anything, I had paved the way for him. This letter is very imprudently shown and spoken of by Mr. Monroe's particular friends, as a proof that he had been the principal agent, in the negotiation. So far, indeed, as it may tend to this object, it is of little moment; because facts and dates are too well known to be contradicted. For instance, it is known to everybody here that the Consul had taken his resolution to sell previous to Mr. Monroe's arrival. It is a fact well known that M. Marbois was authorized, informally, by the First Consul to treat with me before Mr. Monroe reached Paris; that he actually made me the very proposition we ultimately agreed to, before Mr. Monroe had seen a minister, except M. Marbois, for a moment, at my house, where he came to make the proposition; Mr. Monroe not having been presented to M. Talleyrand, to whom I introduced him the afternoon of the next day. All, then, that remained to negotiate, after his arrival, was a diminution of the price; and in this our joint omission was unfortunate, for we came up, as soon as Mr. Monroe's illness would suffer him to do business, after a few days delay, to the minister's offers. There is no doubt that Mr. Monroe's talents and address would have enabled him, had he been placed in my circumstances, to have effected what I have done. But he unfortunately came too late to do more than assent to the propositions that were made us, and to aid in reducing them to form. (Livingston to Madison, Nov. 15, 1803. American State Papers, Foreign Relations, vol. 2, p. 573.)

The credit here claimed by Mr. Livingston is put in question by M. Marbois, who asserts that the preliminary discussions were scarcely entered on, and that their results could not have been anticipated when Mr. Monroe reached Havre. (See Marbois's Louisiana.) This statement seems to be confirmed by reference to Monroe's Memoir, wherein it is stated that, in the first conference between Livingston and Monroe after the latter's arrival in Paris, Livingston said to him: "Only force can give us New Orleans. We must employ force. Let us first get possession of the country and negotiate afterwards."

Marbois narrates that Monroe was not discouraged by the gloomy view entertained by Livingston, but entered upon his conference the next day with zeal. However this may be, Livingston richly merits our everlasting gratitude, and his name will go down with honor with those of Monroe and Jefferson.

THE MAGNITUDE OF THE PURCHASE.

The entire area comprised in the Louisiana Purchase covers 883,072 square miles, and contains 565,166,080 acres. This excludes the area west of the Rocky Mountains, and also that east of the Mississippi, which latter by other treaties is counted as a portion of the Florida cession, and that from Great Britain. The original "Louisiana" contained approximately 571,873,920 acres, and covered 893,553 square miles. The area as given in the "Public Domain" and General Land Office Reports is 756,961,280 acres, or 1,182,752 square miles. This erroneously includes the Oregon country.

The Louisiana Purchase proper embraces the entire States of Arkansas, Missouri, Iowa, Nebraska, North and South Dakota, parts of the States of Minnessota, Kansas, Colorado, Montana, Wyoming, Louisiana, all of the Indian Territory, and part of Oklahoma Territory.

Its area is more than seven times that of Great Britain and Ireland; more than four times that of the German Empire, or of the Austrian Empire, or of France; more than three times that of Spain and Portugal; more than seven times the size of Italy and twice that of Egypt; nearly ten times that of Turkey and Greece; nearly three times that of Sweden and Norway, and nearly six times that of the Japanese Empire. It is also larger than Great Britain, Germany, France, Spain, Portugal and Italy combined. It is about one-fourth less than the area of the thirteen original States.

According to the census of 1890 it had then a population of 11,232,439.

It produced in 1896, according to the reports of the Department of Agriculture, 1,145,137,081 bushels of corn, valued at $191,812,676; 151,395,786 bushels of wheat, valued at $111,488,251; and 260,822,175 bushels of oats, valued at $41,660,266.

The value of real and personal property in 1890 was $3,190,456,461.

The area of public lands disposed of to 1897 amounted to 510,858 square miles, while the public lands remaining unsurveyed aggregated 125,192 square miles. The area unappropriated and subject to entry equals 188,300 square miles.

EARLY OPPOSITION TO ANNEXATION.

In the face of every effort on the part of our Government to acquire valuable foreign territory, there have always been those high in authority and influential in the nation who predicted disaster, belittled the present or prospective value of the proposed acquisition, and discouraged the policy or disputed the constitutional authority for such additions to our domain, whether such extensions were by purchase or voluntary offering without price. It is, however, equally true, and a significant answer, that, without a single exception in our history, every such acquisition has proven immensely valuable, and while it enlarged it also strengthened and enriched our common country. In reviewing the industrial development of the United States and their capacity for the absorption and support of the millions of population which we have invited from other countries, it has been the wonder of the greatest thinkers that, in our numerous acquisitions of such vast areas, we should not have added much more waste and worthless domain to our possessions. With our present knowledge and appreciation of the Louisiana cession, it may be of interest, at this time, to reproduce the exact language used ninety-five years ago by many in this country in severe condemnation of this cession. Jefferson himself suffered bitter detraction and personal ridicule. I append various extracts from speeches in the Senate and House of Representatives in relation to that cession, viz:

Senator Pickering, of Massachusetts, November 3, 1803, said:

It is declared in the third article (of the treaty) that "the inhabitants of the ceded territory shall be incorporated in the Union of the United States." But neither the President and Senate, nor the President and Congress, are competent to such an act of incorporation. He believed the assent of each individual State to be necessary for the admission of a foreign country as an associate in the Union.

Senator Tracy, of Connecticut, said:

We can hold territory; but to admit the inhabitants into the Union, to make citizens of them, and States, by treaty, we can not constitutionally do; and no subsequent act of legislation, or even ordinary amendment to our Constitution can legalize such measures. If done at all, they must be done by universal consent of all the States or partners to our political association.

Representative Griswold, of Connecticut, October 25, 1803, said:

It is not consistent with the spirit of a republican government that its territory should be exceedingly large; for, as you extend your limits you increase the difficulties arising from a want of that similarity of customs, habits and manners so essential for its support.

* * * * * * *

It will not be found either in the report of the secret committee which has recently been published, or in any document or debate, that any individual entertained the least wish to obtain the province of Louisiana; our views were then confined to New Orleans and the Floridas. * * * The vast and unmanageable extent which the accession of Louisiana will give the United States; the consequent dispersion of our population, and the destruction of that balance which it is so important to maintain between the Eastern and Western States, threatens, at no very distant day, the subversion of our Union.

Representative Griffin, of Virginia, said:

He feared the effect of the vast extent of our empire; he feared the effects of the increased value of labor, the decrease in the value of lands, and the influence of climate upon our citizens who should migrate thither. He did fear (though this land was represented as flowing with milk and honey) that this Eden of the New World would prove a cemetery for the bodies of our citizens.

Senator Plumer, of New Hampshire, said:

Admit this western world into the Union and you destroy at once the weight and importance of the Eastern States and compel them to establish a separate, independent empire.

Senator James White, of Delaware, said:

But as to Louisiana this new, immense, unbounded world—if it should ever be incorporated into the Union, of which I have no idea, can only be done by amending the Constitution, I believe it will be the greatest curse that could at present befall us. It may be productive of innumerable evils, and especially of one that I fear to ever look upon. * * * Thus our citizens will be removed to the immense distance of two or three thousand miles from the capital of the Union, where they will scarcely ever feel the rays of the General Government—their affections will become alienated; they will gradually begin to view us as strangers—they will form other commercial connections, and our interests will become distinct. * * And I do say that under existing circumstances, even supposing that this extent of territory was a desirable acquisition, fifteen millions of dollars was a most enormous sum to give.

A STRIKING CONTRAST.

A very few illustrations, in the development of the country embraced within the Louisiana Purchase, will suffice to disprove the gloomy forebodings expressed as to the effect of such an expansion of our empire. I illustrate not with such older States as Louisiana, Iowa, Kansas, Arkansas, Missouri, or even Minnesota, with her 60,000,000 bushels of wheat, ranking her as first among the producers of our nation's wheat yield of 530,000,000 bushels in 1897, not to mention her many other resources, but prefer rather to select the more remote and most recently developed portions of the Louisiana Purchase nearer the Rocky Mountain region, as here the record will read enough like a fairy tale to interest and delight as well as amaze any well-wisher of his country.

The report of the State commissioner of mines of COLORADO for 1897 furnishes the following as the production and value of four metals mined in that State for the year named:

Gold—947,249 ounces	$19,579,636.83
Silver 21,278,202 ounces	12,692,447.47
Copper 9,151,592 pounds	960,917.13
Lead—80,799,778 pounds	2,731,032.49
Total	$35,964,033.92

Colorado's gold yield now exceeds that of California and it is ahead of any other State in this respect. The sheep of Colorado for 1897 were valued at $3,869,445 while the oxen, milch cows and other cattle were valued at $27,177,017 as reported by the Agricultural Department. Her coal yield for 1896 was valued at $3,606,642 as per report of the Geological Survey; and her wheat yield for 1897 aggregated 5,117,000 bushels.

Looking to the neighboring State of Wyoming, we do not find a record for the precious metals, but see a pastoral wealth of vast extent. Her 2,000,000 sheep were valued at $5,714,332 and her oxen, milch cows and other cattle were valued at $17,000,000.

Passing to the adjoining State of Montana—like Wyoming, astride the Rocky Mountains—we observe a marvelous combination of mineral, agricultural and pastoral wealth. The mineral yield of that State for 1897, as reported by the Helena, Montana, assay office, was as follows:

Metals	Customary measures	Quantity	Value
Gold	Fine ounces	217,514.846	$ 4,496,430.92
Silver	do	10,307,446	*21,730,710.03
Copper	Fine pounds	237,188,840	26,798,915.02
Lead	do	25,794,974	928,619.06
Total			$53,954,675.03

*Coinage value.

The mountains and streams of Montana have yielded $7,000,000 of precious metals to the wealth of the world since the advent of those pioneers whose arrival was almost coincident with the discovery there of gold in 1862.

This ranks Montana first in order in silver production as Colorado ranks first in gold. Her copper product also ranked her as first in order for the same year. Her coal yield for 1896 was valued at $2,279,672 as per report of the Geological Survey.

The Montana oxen, milch cows and other cattle were valued at $25,151,882 while her 3,247,641 sheep, valued at $7,804,081 rank her now as first on the roll of the wool-growing States and Territories of the Union. Her wheat yield for 1897 amounted to 2,268,000 bushels.

South Dakota is another instance of marvelous development. Her gold yield in 1897 was $5,300,000 and ranked fourth among the gold-producing States, while her wheat yield was 21,441,248 bushels, valued at $14,794,461.

North Dakota yielded 28,383,552 bushels, valued at $20,981,628. North and South Dakota combined produced nearly one-tenth of all the wheat produced in the United States, and yet these States twelve years ago embraced but one Territory, not thought qualified at that time for statehood.

Perhaps one of the most remarkable evidences of development is that which is exhibited in the case of Oklahoma Territory. Only eight years ago that portion of the Louisiana Purchase was still an Indian reservation—a part of the Indian Territory, and the hunting ground of the tribes therein. So rapid has been the progress since the opening to settlement was formally declared in 1889, that there was a population, as returned by the assessor for 1896, exceeding 275,000 which is now largely increased; and more votes were cast there in that year than are cast in Florida or Delaware. From the last annual report of Governor C. M. Barnes, the total wheat produced for 1897 is found to be 20,000,000 bushels, as per shipments, while the cotton crop marketed amounted to 40,000 bales, and for this year 125,000 bales is the estimate. If this is to mark the advance of eight years, what shall we not expect in twenty years to follow! No other parallel exists—not even in the California days of '49—as to such a growth of population and civil government. Towns and cities were literally built in a night; farms were cleared for the plow; the cereals and esculents planted; orchards prepared; and a system of orderly business inaugurated in thirty days, which in other Territories have required one or more years to accomplish. It is an illustration of what American enterprise and intelligent effort can accomplish under the stimulus of our free institutions.

THE LEWIS AND CLARKE EXPEDITION.

The treaty of the Louisiana cession was concluded April 30, 1803, but even previous to that, Jefferson, while Secretary of State under Washington in 1792, was anxious to explore the country between the Mississippi and Rocky Mountains; he was desirous of extending commercial relations among the Indian tribes of that region and to the more remote West, and of diverting to our own people the traffic of those countries which was then largely monopolized by Canadian and British traders. He communicated with the American Philosophical Society, suggesting that the services of a suitable person be secured to visit the Missouri river, thence cross the Rocky Mountains and proceed as far as the sea; he expressed the hope to the society that a subscription might be raised to aid such an object. Capt. Meriwether Lewis, a captain in the regular Army, and at that time serving in Virginia, heard of this proposition of Mr. Jefferson, and to him offered to undertake such a journey. No means being at hand it was not undertaken. When, however, Jefferson became President the project was still uppermost in his mind, and in a message addressed to Congress January 18, 1803, he recommended that an expedition be authorized at government expense for the purposes mentioned. Congress responded with a generous appropriation and a company was selected under the personal supervision of the President.

The early request of Captain Lewis, who had since then been selected by President Jefferson as his private secretary, was now remembered, and thus his name with that of Captain Clarke is inseparably connected with this world-renowned expedition.

Though the instructions for the expedition were not drafted until June 20, 1803, which was after Louisiana had been ceded to the United States, yet it was before the treaties reached Washington, July 14, 1803.

It is argued that the sending of this expedition to the Pacific is an evidence that Jefferson regarded that country as a part of the Louisiana Purchase, and hence that he desired full information of the possession. This is an erroneous assumption, as it is of record that Jefferson's desire was to improve and extend our traffic with the natives; this is manifest from a reading of the instructions to Lewis and Clarke, which direct that they inform themselves "of the circumstances which may decide whether the furs of those Indians may not be collected as advantageously at the head waters of the Missouri, convenient, as is supposed, to the waters of the Colorado and Oregon or Columbia, as at Nootka Sound or any other point of that coast, and that trade be consequently conducted through the Missouri and United States more beneficially than by the circumnavigation now practiced." They were to hold communication with the various Indian tribes in an endeavor to establish amicable trading relations. When Congress authorized this expedition no information had reached this country that there was even an offer on the part of France to sell us Louisiana. We had confined our attention to the Floridas and to New Orleans, and had expressed no desire for anything westward of the Mississippi. The Lewis and Clarke instructions made it evident that Jefferson was not even considering the country west of the Rocky Mountains as an American possession, since he suggests that the head waters of the Missouri, being convenient to the Columbia river across the mountains, might be selected for the purpose of collecting the furs obtained on the waters of the Columbia and Colorado, instead of transporting them to Nootka Sound on the Pacific, and thence via Cape Horn to the United States—a long and expensive journey. The navigation of the Missouri to its head was a prime object, and this was investigated by Lewis and Clarke, as they proceeded by boats as far as it was possible to go, and their diary is complete on this point. "Through the Missouri and United States" are the words which Jefferson writes to Lewis and Clarke; and they imply that the Missouri was not then understood by him to be in the United States. Therefore it is plain that the expedition of Lewis and Clarke was not even in anticipation of the purchase of any country west of the Rocky Mountains, but for trade purposes only.

This view is confirmed by a letter, from Jefferson to Lewis, written after the cession of Louisiana, which indicates the opinion he then held as to our western boundary, as since established, being the "highlands inclosing all the waters which run into the Mississippi or Missouri directly or indirectly," which then made the Missouri a part of the United States, which it was not when the expedition was formed; the letter also confirms the view as to the original purpose—"the direct water communication from sea to sea formed by the bed of the Missouri and perhaps the Oregon." The following is a portion of Jefferson's letter:

WASHINGTON, *November 16, 1803.*

To Captain LEWIS,

DEAR SIR,—I have not written to you since the 11th and 15th of July, * * * The present has been long delayed by an expectation daily of getting the enclosed account of Louisiana through the press. The materials are received from different persons, of good authority. I enclose you also copies of the treaties for Louisiana, the act for taking possession * * * Orders went from hence signed by the King of Spain and the first consul of France, so as to arrive at Natchez yesterday evening, and we expect the delivery of the province at New Orleans will take place about the close of the ensuing week, say about the 26th instant. * * * At the moment of delivering over the ports in the vicinity of New Orleans, orders will be despatched from thence to those in upper Louisiana to evacuate and deliver them immediately. * * * you must not undertake the winter excursion which you propose in yours of October 3d. Such an excursion will be more dangerous than the main expedition up the Missouri, and would by an accident to you, hazard our main object, which, since our acquisition of Louisiana, interests everybody in the highest degree. The object of your mission is single, the direct water communication from sea to sea formed by the bed of the Missouri, and perhaps the Oregon; by having Mr. Clark with you we consider the expedition as double manned and therefore the less liable to failure; for which reason neither of you should be exposed to risks by going off of your line * * * As the boundaries of interior Louisiana are the high lands enclosing all the waters which run into the Mississippi or Missouri directly or indirectly, with a quarter breadth on the Gulf of Mexico, it becomes interesting to fix with precision by celestial observations the longitude and latitude of the sources of these rivers, so providing points in the contour of our new limits. This will be attempted distinctly from your mission, which we consider as of major importance, and therefore, not to be delayed or hazarded by any episodes whatever.

JEFFERSON'S OBJECT WAS TO SECURE TRADE RELATIONS.

A still further evidence of Jefferson's great object in promoting our trade relations among the Indian tribes west of the Mississippi, which trade extending to the Pacific was then so lucrative to foreign companies, is found in his letter to Astor, five years after the cession, as follows:

WASHINGTON, *April 13, 1808.*

To Mr. JOHN JACOB ASTOR.

SIR,—I have regretted the delay of this answer to your letter of February 27th, but it has proceeded from circumstances which did not depend on me. I learn with great satisfaction the disposition of our merchants to form into companies for undertaking the Indian trade within our own territories. I have been taught to believe it an advantageous one for the individual adventurers, and I consider it as highly desirable to have that trade centred in the hands of our own citizens. The field is immense, and would occupy a vast extent of capital by different companies engaging in different districts. All beyond the Mississippi is ours exclusively, and it will be in our power to give our own traders great advantages over their foreign competitors on this side the Mississippi. You may be assured that in order to get the whole of this business passed into the hands of our own citizens, and to oust foreign traders, who so much abuse their privilege by endeavoring to excite the Indians to war on us, every reasonable patronage and facility in the power of the Executive will be afforded. I salute you with respect.

Whatever the motive may have been which prompted the Lewis and Clarke expedition, it remains as the first exploration of the valley of the Columbia river, from its head to the sea, and forms a substantial link in the chain through which we deduced our rightful claim to that entire country later on. Lewis and Clarke arrived at the mouth of the Columbia river November 15, 1805, where they constructed Fort Clatsop, and remained during the winter of 1805-1806. Upon the return of the expedition, Lewis was very appropriately selected as governor of Louisiana, while later his old associate, Captain Clarke, with equal propriety, was appointed by President Madison, in 1813, governor of the Missouri Territory. As a further evidence of the nation's gratitude munificent grants of public lands were bestowed upon each of these men.

THE FLORIDA BOUNDARIES UNCERTAIN.

The cession of Louisiana from France being now complete, the previous uncertainty as to the western boundary of the Floridas became a prolific source of trouble and anxiety to several nations, and at one time pressed our country to the verge of war. When Talleyrand said to Livingston: "Do you want the whole of Louisiana?" Livingston replied, "No; only New Orleans and the Floridas." He was then of the opinion that France possessed the Floridas. Livingston also convinced Monroe that the Floridas were included in the Louisiana Purchase. President Jefferson was at one time in doubt upon this point. This may seem incredible, but when it is understood that the secret treaty of Paris of October 1, 1800, retroceding Louisiana to France was not made public in full until 1820, when for the first time it appeared in the French and Spanish languages, it can be seen how erroneous impressions were then formed. Mr. Jefferson's letter to Mr. Madison (then Secretary of State), a few months after the cession to us, is of interest on this line:

MONTICELLO, *August 25, 1803.*

DEAR SIR, Your two favors of the 18th and 20th were received on the 21st. * * * I suppose Monroe will touch on the limits of Louisiana only incidentally, inasmuch as its extension to Perdido curtails Florida, and renders it of less worth. I have used my spare moments to investigate, by the help of my books here, the subject of the limits of Louisiana. I am satisfied our right to the Perdido is substantial, and can be opposed by a quibble on form only; and our right westwardly to the Bay of St. Bernard, may be strongly maintained. I will use the first leisure to make a statement of the facts and principles on which this depends * * *

At the time of the retrocession to France it was understood and admitted by all parties that the Floridas were in the physical possession of Spain; the language of the Louisiana sale to our nation reads: "Louisiana, with the same extent that it now has in the hands of Spain, and that it had when France possessed it, and such as it should be after the treaties subsequently entered into between Spain and other States"; and as our negotiators understood that at one time the western part of the Floridas formed a portion of Louisiana, Livingston insisted that our purchase included the same. "What are the eastern bounds of Louisiana?" he asked of Talleyrand. "I do not know; you must take it as we received it," was the reply. "But what do you mean to take?" asked Livingston. "I do not know," said Talleyrand. In the face of this attempted interpretation of the purchase by Livingston, there remained of record in the State Department at Washington his reply of the year before to the French minister, who inquired as to our meaning of the extent of Louisiana, and Livingston replied: "Since the possession of the Floridas by Britain and the treaty of 1763, I think there can be no doubt as to the precise meaning of the terms." He had also urged that Napoleon intercede with Spain for the Floridas. It is true that there was some plausibility in the other view. The French claimed the Iberville by discovery, and, under the rule, could well claim the country drained by it to the eastward.

Following up the Mississippi river from the mouth of the Iberville, the same country along the east of the river was claimed by France and conceded later by Spain. Was it not natural that the eastern bank of the Iberville and the country drained by it should also belong to France? The first attempt to define boundaries was in the treaty of 1763, wherein France agrees with England that the confines between the two countries shall be a line "along the middle of the river Mississippi, from its source to the river Iberville, and from thence by a line drawn along the middle of this river, and the lakes Maurepas and Pontchartrain, to the sea; and for this purpose, the most Christian King cedes in full right and guarantees to his Britannic Majesty, the river and port of Mobile, and everything which he possesses, or ought to possess, on the left side of the river Mississippi, except the town of New Orleans and the island in which it is situated," England in the same treaty became possessed of Florida from Spain, and hence the occasion for defining the lines between France and England. If West Florida belonged to France and was included in the cession by France to England "of everything which he possesses on the left side of the river Mississippi," and subsequently was included in the retrocession of Florida to Spain by England, might it not be claimed by Livingston as being included in the Louisiana Purchase under the terms "with the same extent that it now has in the hands of Spain, and that it had when France possessed it?"

Based on such reasoning, Livingston and Monroe wrote to Madison June 7, 1803:

<small>We consider ourselves so strongly founded in this conclusion that we are of opinion the United States should act on it in all the measures relative to Louisiana, in the same manner as if West Florida was comprised within the island of New Orleans; or, lay to the west of the river Iberville. (State Papers, ii, 564-5.)</small>

President Jefferson was even more radical than Livingston, as his letter to William Dunbar explains, as follows:

WASHINGTON, *March 13, 1804.*

To WILLIAM DUNBAR, Esq.,

DEAR SIR,- Your favor of January 28 has been duly received, * * * We were much indebted for your communications on the subject of Louisiana The substance of what was received from you, as well as others, was digested together and printed, without letting it be seen from whom the particulars came, as some were of a nature to excite ill-will. Of these publications I sent you a copy. On the subject of the limits of Louisiana, nothing was said therein, because we thought it best first to have explanations with Spain. In the first visit, after receiving the treaty, which I paid to Monticello, which was in August, I availed myself of what I have there, to investigate the limits. While I was in Europe, I had purchased everything I could lay my hands on which related to any part of America, and particularly had a pretty full collection of the English, French and Spanish authors, on the subject of Louisiana. The information I got from these was entirely satisfactory, and I threw it into a shape which would easily take the form of a memorial. I now enclose you a copy of it. One single fact in it was taken from a publication in a newspaper, supposed to be written by Judge Bay, who had lived in West Florida. This asserted that the country from the Iberville to the Perdido was to this day called Louisiana, and a part of the government of Louisiana. I wrote to you to ascertain that fact, and received the information you were so kind as to send me; on the receipt of which I changed the form of the assertion, so as to adapt it to what I suppose to be the fact, and to reconcile the testimony I have received, to wit, that though the name and division of West Florida have been retained; and in strictness, that country is still called by that name; yet it is also called Louisiana in common parlance, and even in some authentic public documents. The fact, however, is not of much importance. It would only have been an *argumentum ad hominem*. Although I would wish the paper enclosed never to be seen by anybody but yourself, and that it should not even be mentioned that the facts and opinions therein stated are founded in public authority, yet I have no objections to their being freely advanced in conversation, and as private and individual opinion, believing it will be advantageous that the extent of our rights should be known to the inhabitants of the country; and that however we may compromise on our Western limits, we never shall on the Eastern. * * *

That James Madison, the Secretary of State, also seriously considered this view may be inferred from his instructions to Monroe, of date July 29, 1803, in which he said:

Your inquiries may also be directed to the question, whether any, and how much, of what passes for West Florida, be fairly included in the territory ceded to us by France?

Later on Madison became more positive, and he wrote Monroe, April 15, 1804, that:

It is indispensable that the United States be not precluded from such a construction, [of the treaty] first, because they consider the right as well founded; secondly, and principally, because it is known that a great proportion of the most valuable lands between the Mississippi and the Perdido have been granted by Spanish officers since the cession was made by Spain. These illicit speculations can not otherwise be frustrated than by considering the territory as included in the cession made by Spain,

Monroe received assurances that negotiation for Florida could be entertained for a money consideration, but he replied that our government having purchased that territory once he should not advise that it be bought a second time. Talleyrand had by this time taken a very decided stand against our claim, and now united with Spain for the Iberville and the Mississippi as the eastern boundary.

Pensacola at that time evidently marked the western limits of Florida as they understood it, as then the place was a fort, containing 300 Spaniards from Vera Cruz. Bancroft says in his history (Vol. III, p. 347):

This prior occupation is the reason why afterwards Pensacola remained a part of Florida, and the dividing line between that province and Louisiana was drawn between the bays of Pensacola and Mobile.

This was on the Perdido river, to which President Jefferson again referred, and especially in his letter from Monticello to Mr. Breckenridge:

We have some claims, to extend on the sea coast westwardly to the Rio Norte or Bravo, and better, to go eastwardly to the Rio Perdido, between Mobile and Pensacola, the ancient boundary of Louisiana. These claims will be a subject of negotiation with Spain, and if, as soon as she is at war, we push them strongly with one hand, holding out a price in the other, we shall certainly obtain the Floridas, and all in good time.

As will be seen, Jefferson always insisted that Louisiana properly extended as far eastward as the Perdido river, which is situated between Mobile river and Pensacola. Franquelin's map of 1684, made direct from La Salle's own description of his discovery at the time, gives reason for this position. Louis XIV also claimed all this portion of Florida in his grant to Crozat "in all the lands, possessed by us, and bounded by New Mexico, and by the lands of the English Carolina, all the establishments, ports, havens, rivers, and principally the port or haven of the Isle Dauphine, heretofore called Massacre." This island is westward of the mouth of Mobile Bay. There is also in evidence a letter from De Tonty addressed to La Salle, dated April 20, 1685. In this he expresses his great uneasiness in not having found him, and says: "Two canoes have examined the coast thirty leagues toward Mexico and twenty-five toward Florida." (Falconer's Mississippi, 29.) This was eastward from the mouth of the Mississippi, taking in the coast and mouths of rivers claimed by Spain as West Florida. It also indicates that La Salle's men recognized the country known as Florida, but it was much further east than as claimed by Spain.

THE UNITED STATES DISPOSSESSES SPAIN.

After the cession of 1803 the United States insisted upon a more liberal construction as to boundaries, and attempted a negotiation with Spain at Madrid in 1804. It was contended that the country west of the Perdido river, and west and south to the river Bravo del Norte, with all the intermediate rivers and all the countries drained by them not previously acquired by the United States, should be included in the terms of the purchase of 1803 from France. The Spanish Government denied our rights to any country east and west of the Mississippi, except as to New Orleans with the country on the east immediately contiguous to it, together with the country bordering on the west bank of the Mississippi. It will be seen that as to the country directly east of the island of

New Orleans (which was what Spain previously claimed as West Florida) it was admitted that our nation was entitled to it. The attempt at negotiation, however, failed.

Acting on the popular belief, Congress, in 1812, authorized the general assembly of Louisiana to include in its limits a portion of West Florida, in the face of the claims of Spain. The people of Louisiana persistently claimed it as a part of the Louisiana Purchase. The people within the disputed territory likewise made the same claim, and insisted on separate recognition.

On September 26, 1810, a declaration of independence from Spain was made by the inhabitants of West Florida, and a copy sent to the President of the United States. The first public notice, given to the inhabitants of West Florida of the claim of the United States to the country, was the proclamation of President Monroe of October 27, 1810, which was accompanied by a force that dispossessed the government of Spain. In this proclamation, the President declares that the question of title should remain open for negotiation. Possession was taken by Governor Claibourne, December 7, 1810, and this was followed by the protest of Mr. Morier, British minister to Washington, against the acts of the President.

The Congress of the United States, acting upon the opinion that the cession included the territory west of the Perdido river, on February 24, 1804 (2 Stat., 251), passed an act for laying and collecting duties in the disputed territory. By act of March 26, 1804 (2 Stat., 283), an act was passed erecting Louisiana into two territories, the Territory of Orleans to contain the disputed territory.

In October, 1810, the President issued his proclamation directing the governor of Orleans Territory to take possession of the country as far east as the Perdido.

April 14, 1812 (2 Stat., 708), an act was passed which enlarged the limits of the State of Louisiana, and described lines that include the lands in controversy.

May 14, 1812 (2 Stat., 734), an act was passed annexing the residue of the country west of the Perdido to Mississippi Territory.

March 3, 1817 (3 Stat., 371), Congress included a part of the disputed territory in the Territory of Alabama.

It will thus be seen that the political departments of the government have asserted the claim of the United States to such territory, and the judicial department followed in their footsteps.

An excellent résumé of the various treaties involving the lands in question will be found in the case of Foster v. Neilson (2 Peters, 253).

The opinion of Chief Justice Marshall in this case does not pass directly upon the construction of the treaty of 1803, but decides the case upon the ground that the question of ownership of the disputed territory had already been determined by the political department of the government.

The court says, referring to the various acts of Congress and Executive orders:

> After these acts of sovereign power over the territory in dispute, asserting the American construction of the treaty by which the Government claims it, to maintain the opposite construction in its own courts would certainly be an anomaly in the history and practice of nations. If those depart-

ments which are intrusted with the foreign intercourse of the nation which asserts and maintain its interests against foreign powers have unequivocally asserted its rights of dominion over a country of which it is in possession, and which it claims under a treaty; if the legislature has acted, the construction thus asserted, it is not in its own courts that this construction is to be denied. A question like this respecting the boundaries of nations is, as has been truly said, more a political than a legal question; and in its discussion the courts of every country must respect the pronounced will of the legislature.

The doctrine of this decision has been followed in other cases, notably Garcia v. Lee, 12 Peters, 515; Pollard's Lessee v. Files, 2 Howard, 591; United States v. Reynes, 9 Howard, 127; United States v. Lynde, 11 Wallace, 632.

THE FLORIDA WARS.

In the war between Great Britain and the United States in 1814, General Jackson was sent to Florida to dispossess the British who had captured the forts at Pensacola, and in 1819 the same great general again entered Florida and engaged in a struggle with the Seminole Indians. For two hundred and fifty years the Floridas were the subject of contention. At one time it was by the Spanish, at another by the French, and then by the English; at one time the English governor of Georgia proceeded as far south as St. Augustine in Florida and attempted to take the fort. In later years the Americans figured actively against the Spaniards and Indians. The atrocities perpetrated on the Florida battle grounds, between the Spaniards and the French, and between each of these and the common Indian foe in the earlier years, are perhaps not surpassed in cruelty by those of any other portion of our country. The time was at last at hand when a new and a better destiny was about to have sway. Boundary lines were proving a too feeble barrier to aggressive and progressive Americanism.

THE FLORIDA TREATY.

Active and continuous negotiations followed between our government and Spain; finally that nation, already confronted by many difficulties at home and abroad, acceded to our demands for a cession of the entire Floridas, which, on the 22d of February, 1819, was accomplished. The treaty provided that:

His Catholic Majesty cedes to the United States in full property and sovereignty all the territories which belong to him situated to the eastward of the Mississippi, known by the name of East and West Floridas.

Following our possession General Jackson was made governor of the territory. In after years Mr. Adams, in his Memoirs, referring to this acquisition of territory, says:

I considered the signature of the treaty as the most important event in my life. It was an event of magnitude in the history of this Union.

He took much credit to himself especially for the diplomacy which secured Spain's relinquishment of her claims on the Pacific north of the forty-second degree of latitude, and ranked this of the greatest importance in the settlement of the Oregon question; he held that the Louisiana Purchase gave no claim to the country west of the Rocky Mountains. The area acquired by the United States in this treaty was about 44,639,360 acres, and the total cost, with interest, was $6,489,768. This includes the area between the Perdido and the Mississippi, which was claimed as a part of the Louisiana Purchase. The Public Domain is in error where the area of the Florida cession is given as 59,268 square miles, or 37,931,520 acres. This is properly the area of what is now the State of Florida, the cession having been 69,749 square miles. There has since been included in the State of Louisiana 4,581, Mississippi 3,600, and Alabama 2,300, making a total of 10,481 square miles.

OUR WESTERN LIMIT OF LOUISIANA.

Our nation always claimed, as did France, that the Louisiana Purchase extended westward to the Rio Bravo, because of the settlement made by La Salle when, on his return from France, failing to find the mouth of the Mississippi, he landed on the coast of what is now Texas; therefore, the French always regarded the mouth of the Del Norte as the western limit of Louisiana on the Gulf coast. Popple, an eminent English geographer at that time, conceded this claim and represented on his map the Del Norte as the western limit of Louisiana. The United States on this ground claimed Texas up to 1819, and then abandoned it when Spain ceded to us the two Floridas. It was said at the time that the Spaniards prided themselves on their diplomacy in saving Texas by surrendering Florida; indeed, there is much truth in this boast, when we know how intently resolved our people were to possess the Floridas, and hence we may well infer how ready they also were to relinquish very substantial claims in order to acquire the long-envied Florida possessions; this view is corroborated by reference to President Monroe's message to Congress December 7, 1819, concerning the treaty with Spain in that year, wherein he says:

For territory ceded by Spain other territory of great value (Texas) to which our claim was believed to be well founded was ceded by the United States, and in a quarter more interesting to her.

A quarter of a century later on there was still a vivid remembrance of our old claim to Texas under the Louisiana Purchase, and when in 1844 the annexation of Texas was accomplished, President Tyler in his message to the Senate announcing the negotiation of that treaty said that in event of the approval of annexation—

the Government will have succeeded in reclaiming a territory which formerly constituted a portion, as is confidently believed, of its domain under treaty of cession of 1803 by France to the United States.

THE ANNEXATION OF TEXAS.

The annexation of Texas was even more strenuously opposed, and her possibilities more derided than were those of Louisiana; yet to-day this State occupies a conspicuous place in the sisterhood of States. With her annexation we gained

376,931 square miles to our domain. As we look upon her enterprising people, her prosperous communities, her spacious harbors, her great cotton yield of 2,122,701 bales, valued at $74,322,004, ranking her first among the cotton States (leaving Georgia second and Mississippi third); her nearly 5,000,000 cattle, valued at $73,638,656; her 1,148,500 horses, valued at $19,866,178; her 2,649,014 sheep, valued at $4,409,457, with her annual crops of cereals and fruits, and her rich commerce by land and water—who does not feel proud of the Texan annexation, and hold in veneration the memory of the farsighted and patriotic men who brought it about?

OUR NATION CLAIMS BEYOND THE ROCKIES.

While the expedition of Lewis and Clarke was not conceived originally for the purpose of attaining political ends, yet the disclosures made as to the marvelous country traversed by these explorers aroused a lively interest throughout our nation. When finally, by the treaty of 1819, we secured the claims of Spain north of the forty-second degree of latitude, we more than ever valued Gray's discovery of the mouth of the Columbia and the Astoria settlement, through which alone we deduced an almost incontestable right. At last a national interest had so crystallized about this romantic region westward of the Rockies that soon it was to break forth in the war cry of "Fifty-four, Forty, or Fight."

The restoration of the Astoria settlement (or Fort George), on the Columbia river, to the Americans, pursuant to the first article of the treaty of Ghent, was a most substantial confirmation by Great Britain of the American claim; it was also a stimulus for increased effort toward final recognition of our rights. Negotiations with England were resorted to by our nation, which was represented by Rush and Gallatin, while England was represented by Goulburn and Robinson. Our plenipotentiaries proposed that the line should be drawn from the northwestern extremity of the Lake of the Woods, north or south, as the case might require, to the forty-ninth parallel of latitude, and thence along that parallel westward to the Pacific Ocean. The British commissioners agreed to this line as far west as the Rocky Mountains, but no further. The Americans did not assert that the United States had a perfect right to that country, but insisted that their claim was good at least against Great Britain, and in support of this claim Gray's discovery and our exploration and settlements were relied on. Against these the British negotiators submitted the voyage of Captain Cook and his discoveries, and those of Vancouver and other English navigators; they insisted on an exclusive right based on such claims. They finally indicated, however, a willingness to accept as a boundary the Columbia River, with the joint right at the mouth to a harbor. On such proposals it was impossible to unite, and accordingly it was determined that for ten years there should be a joint occupancy of the country without prejudice to the claims of either nationality. This agreement was signed October 20, 1818, but thus far no treaty had yet been concluded with Spain, although earnest efforts were then in progress. The Spaniards declined to recognize the English or any other claims, but contended for the superiority of their own claims on the ground of Spanish discoveries as well as explorations as far north on the Pacific as the forty-seventh degree of latitude; also by virtue of the expedition of San Juan de Fuca as far back as 1592, and of the voyages of other Spanish navigators later on and long prior to any British explorations or even expeditions.

Spain claimed the Californias and her dominion over that portion of the coast by actual occupancy, while her long-established claims to the territory northward was ably argued by the Spanish minister.

It was noted as significant that Mr. Adams, our Secretary of State, in his negotiations with Spain, refrained from any controversy as to the Spanish claims on the Pacific. It was, however, deemed by our Government an opportune time, while adjusting with Spain our eastern boundaries, also to provide for the strengthening of our claims to territory west of the Rocky Mountains which, by virtue of the discovery of the mouth of the Columbia and its entrance by Captain Gray in 1792, the exploration of the same river from its head waters to the sea by Lewis and Clarke in 1805 and 1806, and by the settlement and occupancy of the Astoria people in 1811, gave to our nation a claim regarded as conclusive against every other nation except Spain, and, as to her, of conceding the discovery and settlement north of the Columbia River, and other discoveries southward on the coast. It was therefore of value, while settling our boundaries, to procure a relinquishment of such claim as Spain might have on that portion of the continent north of California, and this was secured in the treaty of February 22, 1819, and is found in Article III of the treaty, as follows:

> The boundary line between the two countries, west of the Mississippi, shall begin on the Gulph of Mexico, at the mouth of the River Sabine, in the sea, continuing north, along the western bank of that river to the thirty-second degree of latitude; thence by a line due north to the degree of latitude where it strikes the Rio Roxo of Nachitoches or Red River; then following the course of the Rio Roxo westward, to the degree of longitude 100 west from London and 23 from Washington; then crossing the said Red River and running thence, by a line due north, to the River Arkansas; thence following the course of the Arkansas, to its source, in latitude 42 north; and thence by that parallel of latitude to the South Sea. * * * But if the source of the Arkansas River shall be found to fall north or south of latitude 42, then the line shall run from the source due south or north, as the case may be, till it meets the said parallel to the South Sea; * * *

The forty-second parallel of latitude was easily conceded by Mr. Adams to be the northern boundary of the Spanish possessions on the Pacific, because of the undoubted historic evidences not only of discoveries on the coast line, but of actual exploration and settlement by Spaniards to that parallel. North of this parallel the coast line as far as the fifty-sixth degree of latitude was discovered and many parts explored and some named, but these advantages were not followed up by occupation and settlement, and hence in favor of the Americans the Spanish government seemed willing to relinquish its prior claim to all territory north of the forty-second degree.

THE LOUISIANA PURCHASE. 51

We thus closed an account with a troublesome rival. A conclusion was reached, and what has since been known as the Florida treaty was signed. Our southern boundaries were at last agreed upon, together with a cession of Spain's claim to all the country on the Pacific north of the forty-second parallel of latitude, and President Monroe made his announcement of this fact to Congress on the same day.

OUR NATION CONTESTS THE CLAIMS OF ENGLAND ON THE PACIFIC.

Following this treaty a resolution passed the House of Representatives providing: "That an inquiry should be made as to the situation of the settlements on the Pacific Ocean, and as to the expediency of occupying the Columbia river." This was in December, 1820. The report which this resolution invited is in several respects a remarkable document. It claims for our country all the territory from the forty-second degree as far north as the fifty-third degree. It bases our rights not only on discovery and exploration, and through the Florida treaty, but advances our claim for the first time from high authority based on the Louisiana Purchase. The fur trade is referred to as a traffic of great value; a future industry in the fisheries is predicted; trading posts are recommended and immigration favored.

RUSSIA'S CLAIM ACKNOWLEDGED.

In the meantime Russia was taking measures to define its boundaries in the Northwest, and proclamation of the Emperor was made claiming all north of the fifty-first parallel. A joint convention followed between our government and that of Russia, April 5, 1824, at St. Petersburg, by which it was provided that in future our citizens should form no establishments north of 54° 40′ north latitude, and that the Russians should form none south of that parallel. England subsequently entered into an agreement with Russia by which it was stipulated that the boundary line between the possessions of these two powers should be as follows:

Commencing from the southernmost point of the island called Prince of Wales Island, which point lies in the parallel of 54° 40′ north latitude, and between the one hundred and thirty-first and one hundred and thirty-third degree of west longitude (meridian of Greenwich), the said line shall ascend to the north along the channel called Portland Channel as far as the point of the continent where it strikes the fifty-sixth degree of north latitude; from this last-mentioned point the line of demarcation shall follow the summit of the mountains situated parallel to the coast as far as the point of intersection of the one hundred and forty-first degree of west longitude (of the same meridian); and finally, from the said point of intersection, the said meridian line of the one hundred and forty-first degree in its prolongation as far as the frozen ocean. * * * That whenever the summit of the mountains which extend in a direction parallel to the coast from the fifty-sixth degree of north latitude to the point of intersection of the one hundred and forty-first degree of west longitude shall prove to be at the distance of more than ten marine leagues from the ocean, the limit between the British possessions and the line of coast which is to belong to Russia, as above mentioned (that is to say, the limit to the possessions ceded by this convention), shall be formed by a line parallel to the winding of the coast, and which shall never exceed the distance of ten marine leagues therefrom. * * *

RUSSIA SELLS ALASKA TO THE UNITED STATES.

This description was later made the basis in the negotiations between Russia and the United States for the sale of the Russian possessions, known as Alaska, to the United States, and which resulted in the treaty concluded March 20, 1867. Andrew Johnson was then President, and William H. Seward was Secretary of State. The consideration paid by the United States was $7,200,000; and the area acquired was 369,529,600 acres, at a price per acre of about 2 cents. Russia's claim to this country was based on discovery. Captain Behring discovered the mainland of North America on the 18th of July, 1741, and his associate explorer, Tschiriknow, in another vessel discovered many of the islands of the Aleutian Archipelago. Lower down the coast Vancouver made discovery in 1790 of what is now British Columbia, and upon this, England based her claim as far north as the Russian possessions, in opposition to the claim of the Americans that far north based on Captain Gray's discovery of the mouth of the Columbia in 1792.

As another instance of profitable purchase, we are well justified when we refer to our investment in Alaska, and it is amusing to be reminded of the popular opinion entertained when the purchase was made as to its utter worthlessness. In view of recent extraordinary developments in that country it will be of special interest now to quote some of the opinions of eminent statesmen in Congress when the purchase was under consideration by that body, July 1, 1868:

Mr. Orange Ferriss, of New York, said:

> The people of this country do not want these Russian possessions. If submitted to them they would reject the treaty by a majority of millions. Alaska, with the Aleutian Islands, is an inhospitable, wretched, and God-forsaken region, worth nothing, but a positive injury and incumbrance as a colony of the United States.

Mr. Washburne, Wisconsin, said:

> The country is absolutely without value. * * * I tell gentlemen who go for Alaska that Greenland to-day is a better purchase than Alaska. * * *

Mr. Hiram Price, Iowa, said:

> Now that we have got it and can not give it away or lose it, I hope we will keep it under military rule and get along with as little expense as possible. It is a dead loss to us anyway, and the more expense we incur the worse it is for the country and the people.

Mr. B. F. Butler, Massachusetts, July 7, 1868, said:

> If we are to pay for her [Russia's] friendship this amount, I desire to give her the $7,200,000 and let her keep Alaska. * * * I have no doubt that any time within the last twenty years we could have had Alaska for the asking. I have heard it was so stated in the Cabinets of two Presidents, provided we would have taken it as a gift. But no man, except one insane enough to buy the earthquakes in St. Thomas and the ice fields in Greenland, could be found to agree to any other terms for its acquisition to the country.

Mr. Benjamin F. Loan, of Missouri, said:

> The acquisition of this inhospitable and barren waste would never add one dollar to the wealth of our country or furnish homes to our people. To suppose that anyone would willingly leave the

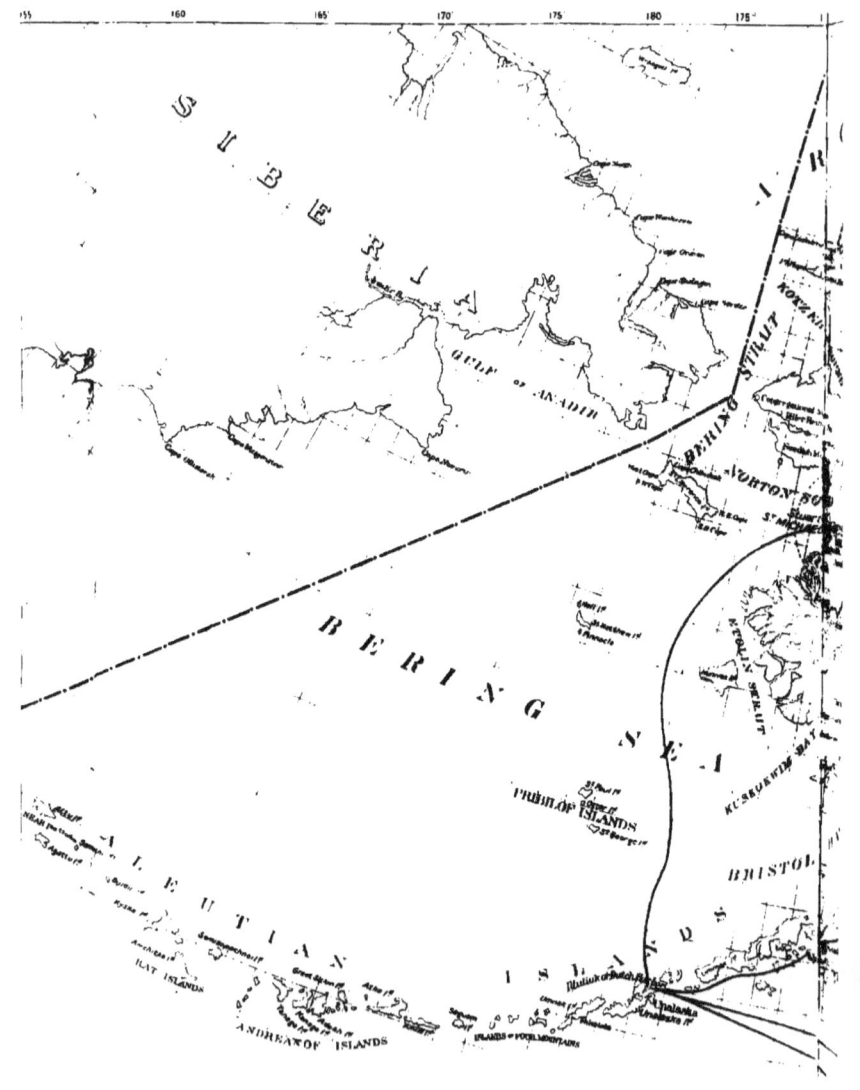

THE LOUISIANA PURCHASE.   53

mild climate and fruitful soil of the United States, with its newspapers and schools, its railroads and commerce, its civilization and refinement, to seek a home among the Aleuts is simply to suppose such person insane.

Mr. Williams, of Pennsylvania, said:

Have the people desired it? [The purchase of Alaska.] Not a sensible man among them had ever suggested it. The whole country exclaimed at once, when it was made known to it, against the ineffable folly, if not the wanton profligacy, of the whole transaction. There is no man here, I think, who would have advised it. I doubt whether there are twenty in this House who would be willing to vote for it now, but for the single reason that the contract has been made.

Mr. Washburne, of Illinois, January 13, 1869 (after the Territory had been purchased, speaking on the bill to provide a government for the same), said:

The accounts which we receive from that Territory of the sickness and suffering of the people who are sent there show conclusively that it will never be inhabited to any considerable extent by white men.

Mr. Ferriss, New York, speaking on the same bill, moved to strike out all after the enacting clause and insert the following:

That the President be authorized to bind the United States by treaty to pay the sum of $7,200,000 to any respectable European, Asiatic, or African power which will accept a cession of the Territory of Alaska.

Such was the unfavorable estimate placed upon this purchase, containing 577,390 square miles of territory. But thirty years have since elapsed. Already such an exhibit is made of the present value as well as of the magnificent possibilities of that region, as to occasion wonder that any doubt should have been entertained as to the advisability of the purchase. The gold production of last year amounted to $2,439,000, while the total gold output since our purchase is estimated to have been nearly $15,000,000, or more than twice the amount paid for Alaska. One single mine, the Treadwell, on Douglas Island, has had an average annual output for some years of $800,000—has paid to its stockholders up to 1896 a total sum of $6,625,945. Since the development of mines on the Yukon and its tributaries fabulous returns may be expected in the next and following years.

As showing the constant increase in the Alaskan gold yield, I present the following figures, furnished by the Director of the Mint:

Production of gold in Alaska since 1880.

Year.	Amount.	Year.	Amount.
1880	$5,951	1889	$800,000
1881	15,000	1890	762,000
1882	150,000	1891	900,000
1883	300,000	1892	1,000,000
1884	200,000	1893	1,010,160
1885	300,000	1894	1,113,550
1886	446,000	1895	1,615,300
1887	675,000	1896	2,055,700
1888	850,000	1897	2,439,000

THE FISH OF ALASKA.

In 1897 the fish product was valued at $2,977,019. Not only salmon, but cod, halibut and herring abound. In 1897, 34 canneries and 14 salteries exported 1,086,650 cases and 15,888 barrels of fish. The tin alone consumed in these canneries is valued at about half a million dollars. In response to an inquiry addressed to the United States Commission of Fish and Fisheries, the honorable Commissioner replied with the following most interesting statement:

> Complying with your request for an approximate statement of the aggregate value of the Alaskan fisheries since the purchase of the Territory, I have based an estimate on the best figures available, although for many of the years only very meager data are obtainable. The total value of these fisheries, excluding the whale fishery prosecuted in Alaskan waters by vessels from San Francisco, appears to have been about $67,890,000. It is possible that this sum is as much as 10 per cent above or below the actual amount.
>
> This opportunity is taken to draw your attention to the remarkable productiveness of the Alaskan waters as regards salmon. During the fifteen years that have elapsed since the inauguration of salmon canning, 7,065,422 cases of salmon, each containing 48 one-pound cans, and 144,000 barrels of salt salmon have been prepared. The gross weight of the fish thus utilized was 610,995,640 pounds, and the market value of the output was about $30,000,000.

THE ALASKAN FUR SEALS.

The fur industry has long been a most lucrative traffic, and China for many years was the place of shipment and market. Captain Cook, in one of his voyages, touched at Unalaska in 1776, where he found the Russians even at that early day. In mentioning this circumstance, he says:

> There are Russians upon all the principal islands between Unalaska and Kamschatka for the sole purpose of collecting furs. Their great object is the sea beaver and otter.

The Alaska Commercial Company possessed a monopoly of the fur-seal industry under a twenty years' lease from our Government, and at its expiration, in 1890, the company had paid into the United States Treasury about $6,000,000. The fur sales by this one company are estimated to have equaled $33,000,000. The North American Commercial Company, under its twenty years' lease, beginning April 1, 1890, paid $340,395, and there is claimed from said company the further sum of $1,134,553 on account of the same lease, for the privilege of taking fur-seal skins on the Pribilof Islands. This one item of fur seals, then, represents a value inuring to the United States Treasury exceeding the entire price paid Russia for all of Alaska.

UNITED STATES LAND DISTRICTS.

Three land districts are now created there, with offices at Sitka, Circle, and Nulatto, and Congress has recently extended the public-land laws, with certain modifications, to that Territory.

This, then, is the Alaskan domain, with an extreme length of 2,000 miles, and larger in area than the thirteen original States, and for this domain our government

William H. Seward

paid 2 cents per acre. This is the Alaska for which the great Secretary Seward suffered much criticism. He lived, however, to ... substantial evidence of the value of his purchase, and confidently predicted ... the future would demonstrate its exceeding importance to our country. In his last days he fondly and often referred to this purchase. A friend at this time said to him: "Mr. Seward, what do you consider the most important measure of your political career?" "The purchase of Alaska," he said, "but it will take the people a generation to find it out."

JOINT OCCUPANCY AND NEGOTIATION.

President Monroe, and after him President Adams, continued to call the attention of Congress to the necessity for military posts on the Pacific within our claim, and each time the discussions in Congress elicited more valuable information respecting the country, its productiveness, its climatic advantages and its future commercial importance to the nation.

The ten-year period, provided for joint occupancy with Great Britain on the Pacific, being about to expire, negotiations between our government and that nation were renewed, and both nations repeated their previous offers, with some modifications by both parties. Mr. Gallatin insisted for the line of the forty-ninth degree, while the British named the Columbia River, with the right of navigation, though they were also willing to add some detached territory from Bullfinches Harbor to the Straits of Fuca, and from the Pacific to Hoods Channel.

The British ultimatum was in the following language:

> The boundary line between the territories claimed by His Britannic Majesty and those claimed by the United States to the west of the Rocky Mountains, shall be drawn due west along the forty-ninth parallel of north latitude to the point where that parallel strikes the great northeasternmost branch of the Oregon or Columbia River—marked in the maps as McGillivrays River—thence down along the middle of the Oregon or Columbia to its junction with the Pacific Ocean, the navigation of the whole channel being perpetually free to the subjects and citizens of both parties.

THE MYSTERY OF THE FORTY-NINTH PARALLEL.

It seems incomprehensible that our early statesmen should differ so radically as to the northern parallel claimed by us as a boundary from the Rocky Mountains to the Pacific, some claiming the forty-ninth parallel and others claiming 54° 40'.

The evidences which I shall present impel me to the conclusion that our inconsistent claims result largely from a mistaken belief as to what occurred pursuant to the treaty of Utrecht. As has been seen by the reading of the letter of Mr. Jefferson to Mr. Mellish, he states that "France and England agreed to appoint commissioners to settle the boundary between their possessions," and that "those commissioners settled it at the forty-ninth degree of latitude." Hence he concludes that such parallel became the northern boundary of Louisiana, this territory being then a possession of France.

As to the original error and the evidences in explanation, I submit the following very interesting data:

[Extract from "Papers respecting the boundary of the United States, delivered to Lord Harrowby September 5, 1804," by Mr. Monroe.]

By the tenth article of the treaty of Utrecht [1713], it is agreed "that France shall restore to Great Britain the bay and straits of Hudson, together with all lands, seas, seacoasts, rivers, and places situate in the said bay and straits which belong thereto," &c.

It is also agreed "that commissaries shall be forthwith appointed by each Power to determine, within a year, the limits between the said bay of Hudson and the places appertaining to the French; and also to describe and settle, in like manner, the boundaries between the other British and French colonies in those parts."

Commissaries were accordingly appointed by each Power, who executed the stipulations of the treaty in establishing the boundaries proposed by it. They fixed the northern boundary of Canada and Louisiana by a line beginning on the Atlantic, at a cape or promontory in 58° 30′ north latitude; thence, southwestwardly, to the lake Mistasin; thence, further southwest, to the latitude 49° north from the equator, and along that line indefinitely.

At the time this treaty was formed France possessed Canada and Louisiana, * * *

By the fourth article of the treaty of 1763, France ceded to Great Britain Canada, Nova Scotia, &c., in the north; and, by the seventh article, the bay and port of Mobile, and all the territory which she possessed to the left of the Mississippi, except the town and island of New Orleans.

By the seventh article it was also stipulated, that a line to be drawn along the middle of the Mississippi, from its source to the river Iberville, and thence along the middle of that river, and the lakes Maurepas and Pontchartrain, to the sea, should be the boundary between the British territory to the eastward, and Louisiana to the west. At that time it was understood, as it has been ever since, till very lately, that the Mississippi took its source in some mountain at least as high north as the forty-ninth degree of north latitude.

By the treaty of 1783, between the United States and Great Britain, the boundary between * * * to the Lake of the Woods, and through that lake to the northwestern point thereof; thence, a due west course, to the Mississippi. * * *

By joining, then, the western boundary of Canada to its northern in the Lake of the Woods, and closing both there, it follows that it was the obvious intention of the ministers who negotiated the treaty, and of their respective Governments, that the United States should possess all the territory lying between the lakes and the Mississippi, south of the parallel of the forty-ninth degree of north latitude. This is confirmed by the courses which are afterwards pursued by the treaty, since they are precisely those which had been established between Great Britain and France in former treaties. By running due west from the northwestern point of the Lake of the Woods to the Mississippi, it must have been intended, according to the lights before them, to take the parallel of the forty-ninth degree of latitude as established under the treaty of Utrecht; * * *

No evidence adopting the forty-ninth parallel.—Mr. Monroe does not give his authority for this assertion respecting the adoption of the forty-ninth parallel by the commissaries under the treaty of Utrecht in 1713, but it is presumed to have been based on instructions from Mr. Jefferson, as he makes the same assertion in his correspondence with others, and especially in his letter of December 31, 1816, to Mr. Mellish, the geographer, to which I have referred.

Mr. Jefferson does not appear to have consulted the opinions of any of the many eminent persons well qualified in every respect to throw light on the subject, or to have searched the archives of any nation, but to have drawn his own conclusions and opinions as to the boundaries of Louisiana, by consulting the few works in his limited library at Monticello, as will be seen by his letters to

Duponceau, Dunbar, Monroe, and others in 180   nd 1804, and then he promulgated his views in the form of a memoir.

The treaty of Utrecht was made principally to define the boundaries between the French and English possessions in North America, and among others the boundary between the French possessions of Canada and Louisiana and the territory of the Hudson Bay Company, then, the only land under British control in that part of the country. The forty-ninth parallel was never mentioned as a boundary in any treaty or convention until this assertion of Mr. Monroe in his letter to Lord Harrowby of September 5, 1804; in fact, its first appearance in any ratified treaty is that of the convention of October 20, 1818.

Both Mr. Jefferson and Mr. Monroe appear to have taken it for granted that because the treaty called for the appointment of commissaries they were really appointed, and had actually marked the line of the forty-ninth parallel, and both insisted on the correctness of their statement. The English authorities, much better informed on this subject, and perfectly aware that the forty-ninth parallel had never before been mentioned as a boundary line, and also aware that the southwest boundary of the Hudson Bay Company's territory was the northern line of Louisiana, quietly jumped at the proposal, and made no attempt to controvert this assertion, made by Mr. Monroe, thereby gaining all the territory between the forty-ninth parallel and the northwest point of the Lake of the Woods (about 36 miles), as the boundary would, by right, have followed the height of land defining the southern limits of the territory of the Hudson Bay Company as given in the original charter.

Jeffery's map of 1762, showing the southern boundary as described above, is reproduced in the "Report on the boundaries of Ottawa, 1873," a report of a special committee appointed by the Dominion Parliament to inquire into the disputed boundaries of Ottawa and Manitoba.

Relative to the statement in regard to the commissaries under the treaty of Utrecht marking the forty-ninth parallel, I have since found the following in the Notes upon the Foreign Treaties of the United States, etc., by John H. Haswell, of the Department of State, January, 1889, page 1324:

> There is no evidence, either in the French or British archives, of the appointment of a boundary commission under the treaty of Utrecht; and in a memorial of the Hudson Bay Company, marked as received August 13, 1719, it is stated that "the running of a line betwixt the English and French territories yet remained to be done." (Mr. Bancroft to Mr. Fish, Sept. 1, 1873. MS. Dept. of State.)

This view is further confirmed by Mr. Greenhow, who says:

> The conclusion would be undeniable, if the premises on which it is founded were correct. The tenth article of the treaty of Utrecht does certainly stipulate that commissaries should be appointed by the governments of Great Britain and France, respectively, to determine the line of separation between their possessions in the northern part of America above specified; and there is reason to believe that persons were commissioned for that object: *but there is no evidence which can be admitted as establishing the fact that a line running along the forty-ninth parallel of latitude, or any other line, was ever adopted, or even proposed, by those commissaries, or by their governments, as the limit of any part of the French possessions on the north, and of the British Hudson's Bay territories on the south.*

It is true that on some maps of northern America, published about the middle of the last century, a line drawn along the forty-ninth parallel does appear as a part of the boundary between the French possessions and the Hudson Bay territories, as settled according to the treaty of Utrecht. But on other maps, which are deservedly held in higher estimation, *a different line, following the course of the highlands encircling Hudson Bay*, is presented as the limit of the Hudson Bay territory, agreeable to the same treaty; and in other maps enjoying equal if not greater consideration published under the immediate direction of the British government, *no line separating those British possessions from Louisiana or Canada is to be seen.*

In the other works, political, historical, and geographical, which have been examined with reference to this question, nothing has been found calculated to sustain the belief *that any line of separation was ever settled or even proposed*, nor has any trace of such an agreement been discovered in the archives of the department of foreign affairs of France, which have been searched with the view of ascertaining the fact.

When Monroe became President he still maintained his theory as to the forty-ninth parallel, and his Secretary of State, Mr. Adams, commenting on our claim, July 22, 1823, said:

> The right of the United States from forty-second to forty-ninth degrees on the Pacific we consider as unquestionable.

Again, in June, 1826, Mr. Clay, being Secretary of State for Mr. Monroe, instructed our minister that he was authorized to offer an *extension* of the line of 49° to the Pacific as a boundary. He said:

> This is our ultimatum, and you may so announce it. We can consent to no line more favorable to Great Britain.

The most pronounced declaration hostile to these repeated views was that enunciated by the Democratic National Convention in 1844, which nominated Mr. Polk for the Presidency. It was unanimously resolved by that convention—

> That our title to the whole of Oregon is clear and unquestionable; that no portion of the same ought to be ceded to England or any other power.

And it was urged against Mr. Clay that in 1826, while Secretary, in his instructions to Mr. Gallatin, he first declared that Great Britain had not, and could not make out "even a colorable title to *any* portion of the northwest coast," yet in the same communication he had authorized Mr. Gallatin to "propose the annulment of the convention of 1818 and the extension of the line on the parallel of 49° from the eastern side of the 'Stony Mountains' to the Pacific, together with the free navigation of the Columbia."

Mr. Polk was pledged to retain the whole of the Oregon territory, but when he became President he, too, felt obliged to follow his predecessors, though not conceding to Great Britain any right whatever. He, however, would not agree to allow the free navigation of the Columbia. He considered that all offers by our negotiators of the forty-ninth parallel could not, with any hope of success, be enlarged by him. Three separate attempts had been made under Presidents Monroe and Adams, in 1818, 1824, and 1826, and all on the line of the forty-ninth degree, and Tyler repeated the offer in 1843. Polk accepted this parallel as a boundary—not as a right, but as a compromise. In his message to Congress in 1845 he submitted such views.

When the treaty of 1846 was before the Senate for ratification Mr. Benton expressed the view that the forty-ninth parallel was ours as a matter of right, as it was also a line of convenience between the two nations. He argued that it parted the two systems of water—those of the Columbia and those of the Fraser; that it also conformed to the actual discoveries and settlements of both parties. There was not on the face of the earth, he said, so long and so straight a line or one so adapted to the rights of the parties and the features of the country. He insisted that the forty-ninth parallel had been agreed upon by the commissioners :

> This boundary was acquiesced in for a hundred years. By proposing to follow it to the summit of the Rocky Mountains, the British Government admits its validity; by refusing to follow it out, they became obnoxious to the charge of inconsistency.

To those who believed as did Mr. Benton on this line, and who also believed that the Louisiana Purchase extended to the Pacific, this position was consistent; but to those who claimed that our title to the country westward of the Rocky Mountains was derived through discovery, or through the relinquishment of the Spanish claim, or both, the forty-ninth parallel could only be accepted as Mr. Polk held, as a compromise, but not as a fixed right, and such view is without any original authority to sustain it, so far as it may be derived through the treaty of Utrecht. If our right west of the Rocky Mountains was obtained through Captain Gray's discovery, and through the relinquishment of the Spanish claim, then, as against Great Britain, our line should have been 54° 40′, and all reference to previous adjustments east of the Rocky Mountains on the line of 49° for boundary between the English and French possessions could have no application to the country west of those mountains. France had no possessions in that portion of the continent. Even though commissioners had settled a boundary, as Mr. Monroe believed, their action could not have had in contemplation country not in possession of France.

CONTINUED NEGOTIATION.

The second negotiation on the line of the forty-ninth parallel, in which Mr. Gallatin appeared for the United States, progressed, and great interest was manifested by the people of both nations.

Again the parties failed to agree, and again another extension of time was allowed for joint occupancy, this time, however, for an indefinite period, either party being at liberty to abrogate the extension by giving one year's notice. The United States closed this second attempt by adhering to the claim for all the country from the forty-second to the forty-ninth degrees of north latitude. The debate attending the conference was marked by a high order of ability, the diplomatic skill, clear logic, and industrial research shown by Mr. Gallatin being especially conspicuous. The conference was followed by a long interval of time, during which little was said or done in Congress in reference to the disputed territory. Among the people, however, much advance was quietly being made. Exploring parties, trading companies and missionaries were each year finding their way by water and by land to the country. Associations were formed in various States to emigrate to what now became more generally known as the "Oregon country." These people in turn opened up communication with those left behind, thereby adding much to the general knowledge of the country and creating renewed interest in that region; this renewal of interest brought additional influence upon Congress from the more western States in the form of petitions from legislatures and public assemblages demanding action on the part of the government and a more aggressive assertion of our rights to the country claimed.

HALL J. KELLEY'S IMMIGRATION SCHEMES.

Perhaps no one at so early a date did so much to arouse public attention to Oregon as did Hall J. Kelley, a graduate of Harvard University, of pious yet suspicious temper, and a lover of travel and exploration. He was peculiar in many characteristics, and was thought by many at the time to be a mere enthusiast and dreamer, yet he was a man of learning, undaunted courage, and inflexible determination. His self-sacrifices and adventures read at the present time more like romance, as his observations and conclusions pointing to the future of the country seem like prophecy. As early as 1815 he became active in his attention to that disputed domain. He was constantly acquiring information from the trapper, the explorer, and the navigator. He proclaimed the supreme right of our country to that land, and believed it a duty to acquire it, not only for its value in a commercial sense and for expansion of American empire, but also for the humanitarian work of Christianizing the Indian. He organized a land expedition in 1828, which failed because of lack of confidence in the success of the undertaking. This was followed later by an attempt to fit out an expedition by sea, with a view of locating a colony on Puget Sound. This also failed. In 1829 he incorporated a society for Oregon immigration. Lands were to be cultivated, towns built, ports established, trade opened by water to the islands and to the Orient, and schools and churches were to be encouraged. He lectured and printed much information on Oregon, and was the author of a variety of books and pamphlets on his favorite subject. A circular was published and distributed far and wide; it contained a description of the country and of the routes of travel, with a glowing outlook for the future. Congress was memorialized to aid his undertaking, and prominent men connected with the Government were importuned to cooperate with him in securing a grant of

25 square miles of land in the Columbia River Valley for colonial purposes. In 1834 he reached Oregon, after long and most adventuresome travel, and there, in that promised land, suffered in ways which clouded the happiness of his after life, which continued until the ripe age of 85 years. On his return his published accounts of Oregon were remarkably accurate; and his suggestions for improving the entrance of the Columbia river, with information as to the shipbuilding facilities of Puget Sound, and the timber, minerals, climate and soils of Oregon, were all verified by closer observation in later years. Senators Linn and Benton, in their long struggle in the United States Senate for our title to Oregon, had frequent occasion to consult Hall J. Kelley as an authority on that country. He induced many persons to go there, who in turn encouraged others, and substantial benefits followed, due directly and indirectly to his efforts. He lived to behold the growth of a mighty empire, and the formation of States and Territories, from what was a comparatively unexplored and unknown region when he first published to the world a narrative of its then incredible resources, with a foresight of its magnificent destiny. It may, indeed, be true, as was said of him, that he was more capable of forming grand schemes than of carrying them to a successful issue, yet history owes to his memory the credit of acknowledging the invaluable aid which he rendered his country by his unselfish devotion and lifelong labors.

THE WILKES EXPLORING EXPEDITION.

Still later came the publications by the Government of Captain Wilkes's exploring expedition, which reached Oregon in the spring of 1841. To Wilkes was intrusted the command of a squadron composed of the sloops of war *Vincennes* and *Peacock*, the brig *Porpoise*, the ship *Relief*, and tenders *Sea Gull* and *Flying Fish*. Eminent scientists accompanied the expedition. Surveys were made of the Columbia river, and most valuable scientific and general information obtained of the country and of the aboriginal inhabitants, as well as of the British fur-trading companies, all of which, being published officially and under the supervision of the government, attracted greater attention to the publications. The reports covered a wide range of subjects, and being more in detail than the observations by Lewis and Clarke, thirty-five years before, may be said to be the most valuable and reliable of any official information obtained of the Oregon country. Numerous books in various languages were the result of this expedition, though it should also be said that other countries than Oregon were included in Wilkes's expedition, and were described in his very interesting reports.

President Tyler, in his message to Congress December 7, 1842, in referring to the Oregon question, assured that body he should "not delay to urge on Great Britain the importance of its early settlement." Bills were introduced extending the laws of the United States over that country, conferring grants of lands upon settlers, and establishing a line of forts, with other protective assurances.

AMERICAN SETTLEMENTS ENCOURAGED.

Much discussion arose in the consideration of these measures in Congress. Senator Benton, as before mentioned, based our right to Oregon on the Louisiana Purchase, arguing that it could be construed to establish the forty-ninth parallel as our northern boundary and hence to include this territory, as he asserted this boundary to have been fixed by commissaries appointed pursuant to the treaty of Utrecht.

Senator Benton, in that memorable speech, insisted that occupancy would accomplish more than treaties. He said:

> I now go for vindicating our rights on the Columbia, and, as the first step toward it, passing this bill and making these grants of land which will soon place thirty or forty thousand rifles beyond the Rocky Mountains.

The Senate in 1843 passed the bill, introduced in that body, containing the guaranties as to governmental protection, and land grants to individuals who should settle in that country, with assurances as to immediate occupation by the General Government. These inducements were sufficient. Without waiting for the enactment of this bill into law, large bodies of people commenced their march for Oregon and, uniting at a point in Missouri, in June, 1843, previously agreed upon, they traveled together across the continent. They comprised the first large body of American citizens to reach the disputed territory. To this movement, more than to any previous one, may we credit the first real promise for the permanent occupation of the country under the American flag, with the pledge of the nation to defend it at all hazards. The spirit of these daring men and pioneers, and their heroic courage in asserting our rights in the far-distant Oregon, produced for them a universal feeling of admiration throughout the country, and with it an expression of opinion that the moment had arrived when war should take the place of debate, and that further to delay the assertion of our rights would be national dishonor.

"FIFTY-FOUR, FORTY, OR FIGHT."

As President Jefferson, in 1803, was pressed on by the appeals from the planters on the banks of the Mississippi, and the earnest demands of his impatient countrymen everywhere, so was President Tyler, in 1843, moved to serve a final notice upon England that further negotiation must cease, and he earnestly recommended to Congress the immediate establishment of fortified places along the route to Oregon. In his annual message of December 5, 1843, he proclaimed it as the voice of the nation to defend all of the country north of latitude 42° and south of 54° 40' on the northwest coast. President Tyler evidently did not believe that the forty-ninth parallel had ever been established by any commission, or if so, he did not believe it should apply to the boundary west of the Rocky Mountains.

This was at last a language which could not be mistaken, and it accelerated the final terms of the conference which had for the third and last time convened in

JAMES K. POLK

negotiation of the Oregon question. When President Polk soon afterward succeeded President Tyler, he, while reiterating his former position as to our right, indicated his intention to stand by the modified offer of the forty-ninth parallel purely as a compromise, and also announced the opinion that our nation should terminate the joint occupancy and give England the necessary one year's notice. Demonstrations in approval of this determination to end the uncertainty were everywhere heard. War now seemed inevitable and preparations followed. This evidence of popular feeling, following the very decided tone of Tyler and Polk, was the best reminder to the British that no more concessions would be made by our government. Finally the settlement came in the offer of Britain to accept the forty-ninth parallel and the Straits of Fuca for the northern boundary of our nation, and this being accepted the treaty was ratified June 15, 1846. Thus ended one of the most memorable and long-continued negotiations, and one in which some of the most eminent statesmen of both countries participated. Our own nation selected such men as Gallatin, Webster, Calhoun and Buchanan. The arguments submitted by our negotiators evinced the greatest learning, ingenuity and patient research.

OREGON ADMITTED AS A TERRITORY.

President Polk, who was at all times the earnest friend of Oregon, and who was elected, as before stated, on a platform which firmly asserted the right of our nation to that entire region, was now extremely anxious that a territorial form of government should be extended over it during his administration.

In his annual message to Congress in 1846, and in 1847, he strongly recommended this action. On May 29, 1848, he submitted to both Houses of Congress a special message again urging attention and reminding the nation's lawmakers of the memorials of settlers in the Columbia river valley, of their exposed condition, and of the pressing necessity which required that mounted men should immediately be called into service.

Even in his first message to Congress he expressed his solicitude for these exposed pioneers. He said:

It is much to be regretted that while under this act British subjects have enjoyed the protection of British laws and British judicial tribunals throughout the whole of Oregon, American citizens in the same territory have enjoyed no such protection from their government. At the same time the result illustrates the character of our people and their institutions. In spite of this neglect they have multiplied, and their number is rapidly increasing in that territory. They have made no appeal to arms, but have peacefully fortified themselves in their new homes by the adoption of republican institutions for themselves, furnishing another example of the truth that self-government is inherent in the American breast and must prevail.

Bills were introduced in Congress providing a territorial form of government, and affording such other relief as had been recommended. Much delay ensued over the question, so common at that time in the admission of States and Territories, as to whether slavery should or should not be prohibited.

The objectionable clause in the Oregon bill to many was that which recognized and extended to the new territory the principle of the ordinance of 1787 excluding slavery, which ordinance was also in harmony with the legislation of the provisional government of Oregon interdicting slavery. This clause in the bill was as follows:

> That the inhabitants of said Territory shall be entitled to enjoy all and singular the rights, privileges, and advantages granted and secured to the people of the territory of the United States northwest of the river Ohio by the articles of compact contained in the ordinance for the government of said Territory, on the 13th day of July, 1787, and shall be subject to all the conditions and restrictions and prohibitions in said articles of compact imposed upon the people of said territory.

The objection urged against this principle was crystallized in the strong words of John C. Calhoun, in his speech on the bill, in which he said:

> There are three questions involved: First, the power of Congress to interfere with persons emigrating with their (slave) property into the State; second, the power of the territorial government to do it; and third, the power of Congress to vest such a power in the Territory.

This was the issue, and around it waged the struggle. Should it be free, or should it be slave territory? The most eminent statesmen of our nation participated in the debates in this memorable contest. Webster, Cass, Calhoun, Douglas, Benton, Crittenden, Hale, Houston, McClernand, Collamer, Corwin of Ohio, Butler of South Carolina, Bell of Tennessee, Davis of Mississippi, and Mason of Virginia—all Senators—assumed a leading part. Hannibal Hamlin, afterwards Vice-President, was a Senator at that time.

In the House of Representatives, among those then and since eminent before the country and voting on the passage of the bill, were John Quincy Adams of Massachusetts, Abraham Lincoln and John Wentworth of Illinois, Andrew Johnson of Tennessee, Joshua R. Giddings of Ohio, David Wilmot of Pennsylvania, Robert Toombs and Alexander H. Stephens of Georgia. Of these distinguished men one had been previously and two were afterwards Presidents of the United States. It may also be mentioned, as of some interest, that President Taylor offered to Abraham Lincoln the governorship of the Territory to succeed Governor Lane, and that the honor was declined.

The fight was a hard and a long one, but the end came gloriously, and Oregon with its vast domain was constituted a Territory of the United States on the 14th day of August, 1848, with all the privileges and benefits which follow such conditions in the political relations of newly admitted territories. The vote of admission was also conclusive upon the question of slavery, and free soil was proclaimed as a heritage for the new empire west of the Rocky Mountains.

Of all the eminent statesmen who were true and tried in the long contest for supremacy of American rights upon the far-distant Oregon, none should be longer or more gratefully remembered by the people of the Pacific northwest than Thomas H. Benton.

Thomas H. Benton

THOMAS H. BENTON.

He was for thirty years in the United States Senate from the State of Missouri, and was one of the strong and early advocates of the Oregon country. His influence all the way through, and in the last trying ordeal preceding the admission of Oregon into the Union as a Territory, was most effective. He was the earliest friend of a railroad to the Pacific, and was largely instrumental in securing governmental surveys with a view to ascertaining the feasibility of railway construction to that remote land. He was always prominent in explorations in the far West, and in encouraging overland transit to the Pacific. His prediction as to the traffic which would meet at the mouth of the Columbia river— coming and going between the Occident and the Orient—has been verified in a surprising degree. As far back as 1820 he was the author of many valuable contributions to the public press on the resources of the great West. He was at all times an ardent annexationist, having taken an active part in reference to the annexation of Texas. His influence with President Polk had much to do in deciding that distinguished President's attitude in reference to the acceptance of the boundary line west of the Rocky Mountains on the parallel of the forty-ninth degree. His participation in all the discussions attending the acquisition of the Mexican territory was active, and his aid invaluable. In the history of western development his name will live long as one of its most able and successful advocates.

OREGON PROVISIONAL GOVERNMENT.

The pioneers of the West.—Gen. Joseph Lane, of Mexican war fame, was appointed by President Polk governor of the new Territory, and on the 3d day of March, 1849, he reached Oregon City, and there, unfurling the Stars and Stripes over that westerly confine of our Republic, he assumed the duties of his office and proclaimed the laws of the United States to be in force. Governor George Abernethy, who had so wisely and so conscientiously served as provisional governor for the four preceding years, cheerfully relinquished his authority to the chosen representative of our great nation. During those four years of anxiety a thoroughly organized government had been successfully maintained, laws were enacted by an orderly elected legislative assembly and construed by a judicial tribunal carefully selected and composed of men of recognized ability and integrity. Taxes were imposed and revenues collected without difficulty, while the strength of the pioneer government was severely tested by wars with the hostile Indians, when troops were raised, officers commissioned, discipline maintained, battles fought and victories won. Here was an independent State and a voluntary government 3,000 miles remote from the capital of our nation, which had long been petitioned and implored for its protecting ægis. Our history has afforded no loftier illustration of the capacity of the American citizen for self-government, because no other people on this continent, for so long a period, suffered the same isolation, endured the same privations, or so patiently and uncomplainingly faced the same responsibilities and so honorably and successfully fulfilled them, as these builders of American empire west of the Rocky Mountains. Their provisional government is as splendid a monument to their administrative ability as the example of their heroic struggles and patriotic devotion is an inspiration and a blessing to all who shall come after them. The annals of pioneer civilization may be searched in vain for names more honored or more worthy of remembrance by a grateful people than those of McLoughlin, Whitman, Abernethy, Lane, Thurston, Nesmith, Williams, Applegate and Deady. Some of them have ornamented the highest legislative councils of our nation, and some of them the judiciary; some achieved fame on the battlefield or as self-denying missionaries, while still others filled the measure of their ambition in the provisional and territorial governments. Many, too, there were who liberally extended the hand of charity to the needy, and in the hour of danger heroically marched to the rescue of the belated, the wayworn, and the often imperiled emigrant; but of them all the generous and knightly deeds of old John McLoughlin are of lasting and most precious memory.

THE EXTENT OF THE OREGON COUNTRY.

The Oregon country now embraces the States of Oregon, Idaho, Washington and parts of Montana and Wyoming.

Its area is more than two and one-third times that of Great Britain and Ireland; more than two and one-half times that of Italy; more than one-third larger than either France, the German or the Austrian Empire; one-quarter larger than Spain and Portugal; larger than the German Empire, Switzerland, Denmark, Belgium and the Netherlands combined; larger than Japan, the Philippines and the Hawaiian Islands; four times larger than the New England States; more than two and one-half times larger than New York, New Jersey, Pennsylvania, Delaware and Maryland combined; more than two and one-fifth times larger than Ohio, Indiana and Illinois; larger than the total area of Virginia, North and South Carolina, Kentucky and Tennessee; and larger than the States of Texas, or California and Nevada.

The population is now in excess of 1,000,000.

The value of real and personal property in 1890 amounted to $423,887,065. Since then it has increased a large per cent, while the agricultural, mining and lumber interests have grown to vast proportions.

The public lands disposed of prior to 1897 equal an area of 80,118 square miles.

Three great transcontinental railways now cross the lofty Rocky Mountain range and unite the upper Mississippi and the Great Lakes with the waters of the Columbia, while still another railway commencing at New Orleans, once the capital of the original Louisiana province, and reaching over the State of Louisiana around from the south through Texas, New Mexico, Arizona and California, crosses the forty-second parallel of north latitude, passing through Oregon, until it finds

a terminus at the city of Portland on the tide waters of the Pacific Ocean.
Flourishing cities, towns, and villages, well-cultivated farms, vineyards and
orchards, and manufacturing, mining and commercial enterprises are found at
frequent intervals, often in continuous lines, along these vast distances of travel;
and yet there are those still living who have seen that great expanse of country
when it was comparatively unknown, the greater portion of which having been
noted on the maps of our schoolboy days as "Desert" or "Unexplored." By
many it was regarded as a worthless waste. So late as January, 1843, when our
nation's claim to the Oregon country was still being considered, Mr. McDuffie, a
distinguished Senator, in a speech delivered in the United States Senate, said:

What is the nature of this country? Why, as I understand it, 700 miles this side of the Rocky Mountains is uninhabitable; a region where rain seldom ever falls; a barren, sandy soil; mountains totally impassable. Well, now, what are we going to do in this case? How are you going to apply steam? Have you made anything like an estimate of the cost of a railroad from here to the Columbia? Why, the wealth of the Indies would be insufficient. Of what use will this be for agricultural purposes? Why, I would not for that purpose give a pinch of snuff for the whole territory. I thank God for His mercy in placing the Rocky Mountains there.

A SPLENDID EMPIRE.

Had such pessimistic statesmen prevailed we can now realize what would
have been lost to our country in a failure to assert our rightful claim to this domain.
I have adverted to the marvelous productions in agriculture, and other resources
of the entire region west of the Rockies. It may be of interest to single out
the individual States, which now form the group once embracing the Oregon
country, and credit each with a few of the items which enter into its industrial
development. The Statistical Abstract of the United States for 1897 enables us
to verify some most interesting facts:

Oregon, the mother of the group, makes a magnificent industrial showing,
and a few productions must illustrate for all. Her gold yield in 1897 is valued at
$1,354,500, as estimated by the Director of the Mint, but as unofficially reported
here is $3,000,000. The foreign and domestic exports in 1897, as shown by the
customs reports, equaled about $7,016,368, while the free and dutiable imports
amounted to $1,640,099. Her wool clip for the same year equaled 18,440,850
pounds; the sheep numbered 2,682,779, and were valued at $4,451,150, ranking
her as third in number of sheep among the wool-growing States and Territories.
The oxen and other cattle were valued at $11,957,188, horses at $3,989,854, and
milch cows at $2,689,449. The salmon fisheries and canneries reported a gross
output for the same year valued at $1,231,591. The wheat yield in 1897 equaled
18,155,000 bushels, valued at $13,071,000, while the hay product was valued at
$8,431,550. The Oregon timber, like that of Washington and California, is
noted for its mammoth size and superior quality as well as for its quantity. In
four counties alone, along the coast, the standing timber is estimated to contain
56,000,000,000 feet, B. M. The bank clearings for Portland will best illustrate
the commercial importance and marvelous growth of that metropolis of less than
100,000 inhabitants, and also indicate the progressive spirit which animates the

business communities tributary to this great shipping mart of the Pacific Northwest. In 1897 these clearings amounted to $73,340,000, while the wholesale trade for the same year is shown to have equaled in value $75,000,000. (See holiday edition *Oregonian*, January, 1898.) The lumber, coal, fruit, hop and numerous other products could be added to swell the grand total, and, when to this we further add the value of improved farm land, the value of the mines, forests and manufacturing plants, and the wealth of the towns and cities, we should call forth the departed shades of the old Senators to apologize for their sneering estimates of this wonderland for which they would not give a "pinch of snuff" in 1843.

Washington, the second State of the group, is not far behind the first. The domestic and foreign exports of Puget Sound, in Washington, which in 1883 amounted to $1,770,219, had increased in 1897 to $11,864,925, while the total free and dutiable imports for that year equaled $7,066,131. These exports exceed those from many of the great ports on the Atlantic, such as Charleston, Wilmington, Mobile and Pensacola. The bank clearings of the two leading cities will perhaps afford an excellent index of the industrial activity. In 1897 the clearings for Seattle represent $36,050,000, while those for Tacoma represent $28,910,000. The timber cut in the State of Washington, in 1892, for manufacturing purposes amounted to 1,440,135,000 feet, of which 275,000,000 was in laths and shingles. There was sold in that single year to Australia, Hawaii and South America 100,000,000 feet of lumber. That a proper conception may be formed of the productive forest area of Washington, it may be stated, on the authority of the Department of Agriculture, that the standing timber (mainly Douglas spruce) equals 410,000,000,000 feet and covers 23,500,000 acres. Dwelling still further upon this State, it may be said to rank eleventh among the wheat-growing States of the Union, having produced in 1897, 20,124,648 bushels, valued at $13,684,761. In the same year Washington had oxen and beef cattle valued at $5,436,952, milch cows valued at $3,109,677, horses valued at $4,163,817, and sheep valued at $1,622,446. The gold output in 1897 amounted to $449,600, and the silver production to $313,900.

Idaho—the Gem of the Mountains—the latest of the northwest group, and which was admitted into the Union as a State so late as July 3, 1890, only eight years ago, also presents a most creditable showing. Her gold yield in 1897 was valued at $2,125,300, and her silver at $7,103,300, while her lead output was large, valued at $3,500,000, as per estimate of the Director of the Mint. The value of her oxen and other cattle in 1897 was $6,500,000, and the sheep $3,612,313. Her wheat yield in 1897 amounted to 2,707,672 bushels.

OUR MEXICAN PURCHASE.

A still further illustration of timely and profitable acquisition of territory is that represented through the treaty of Guadaloupe Hidalgo with Mexico, February 2, 1848, following, and growing out of the Mexican war.

THE LOUISIANA PURCHASE.   69

This brought to us 522,568 square miles, or 334,443,520 acres, to which should be added the Gadsden Purchase five years later, covering 45,535 square miles, and embracing an area of 29,142,400 acres. From these we have since formed five great political divisions, viz, the States of California, Nevada, Utah, the Territories of New Mexico and Arizona in part, and a small portion of what is now Colorado and Wyoming. Merely to mention CALIFORNIA is to emphasize the enormous value of the acquisition. She has contributed to the nation, and to the world's supply of gold, since 1848, an excess of $1,309,490,917, as shown by the United States Mint returns for successive years. In a single year (1853) her gold output was valued at $65,000,000. Her precious mineral product was the marvel of the world, and exercised a material influence in the relation of the money metals among the nations. With such an exhaustive and continuous outpour of her golden metal during fifty years of her status as an American community, she still maintains a bounteous offering, and though no longer the largest producer, her yield last year amounted to $15,871,000. The gold product of the United States, in 1897, reached a total of $59,210,795, more than one-fourth the entire gold production of the world, and placed our nation ahead of any other country in yield. We owe this proud eminence to our foresight and wise policy of annexation; without it our land of gold would have continued to remain the possessions of foreign powers. California has discovered also that her wealth is not alone in her minerals, but that agriculture, horticulture, and animal industry are within her capabilities, and her splendid showing attests this. Her 20,000,000 bushels of barley, worth $11,000,000, ranks her as first in barley production. This State is also first in citrous products. Her wheat product, in 1897, was 39,394,020 bushels, valued at $26,887,000, ranking her fifth in order among the wheat-growing States. Her hay product is valued at $24,444,000, and fourth in order. Her wheat value is now almost twice that of her gold yield. Her sheep are valued at $5,785,915; cattle, including milch cows, at $25,137,835, and her horses and mules at $14,246,765. Her wine product is 30,000,000 gallons, beet sugar 65,000,000 pounds, raisins 64,000,000 pounds, prunes 82,000,000 pounds, and oranges 10,250 carloads. The redwood along the coast range alone is estimated to contain 25,000,000,000 feet, B. M., and the mills manufacture enormous quantities of lumber and employ large numbers of her people.

The remainder of our Mexican purchase also makes an excellent exhibit:

Utah mined $1,805,988 of gold and $11,413,463 in silver last year. Her cattle and milch cows were valued at $7,056,000, while her sheep were valued at $4,144,863. The copper output in 1896 amounted to $376,500, and the lead output to about $2,000,000. Her wheat yield in 1897 was 3,190,740 bushels.

Nevada had a gold yield in 1897 of $2,468,000, and a silver yield of $905,310. Her sheep were valued at $1,206,467, and the cattle and horses at $5,264,000.

New Mexico's gold and silver yield did not exceed $681,239, but she makes her record at present in cattle, valued at $12,329,397, and her sheep, valued at $5,364,284. The wheat yield in 1897 amounted to 4,282,848 bushels.

Arizona possesses a value in cattle of $7,807,000, and in sheep of $1,773,734; her gold yield amounted to $2,700,000, and her silver product to nearly as much. The output of copper for Arizona in 1896 amounted to $7,840,505.

For all this splendid empire from Mexico, embracing three whole States, portions of two others, and almost two entire Territories, the purchase price was $15,000,000!

TOTAL SILVER OUTPUT.

Here it may be proper to add that the total silver production of the United States in 1896 was valued at $76,069,000, and of this 95 per cent was mined in six divisions: Colorado, Montana, Utah, Idaho, Nevada and Arizona. This only emphasizes in another way the forcible manner in which we are reminded of the benefits which have accrued to our nation through the policy of annexation and territorial expansion. Americans now own this wealth, and an American—not a foreign—flag floats over this entire domain of precious metal output.

TOTAL COST OF ANNEXATIONS.

The grand total of the sums paid for our foreign acquisitions amounts to $52,200,000, a sum less than the value of one year's output of Montana's minerals, of Minnesota's annual wheat yield, or of the cattle and hay product of California for one year.

IMPERFECT STATISTICS.

In justice to the different States and Territories whose leading resources have been briefly mentioned, it should be said that the statistics quoted are in every instance believed to represent less than the actual quantities and values. The government's statistician makes record only of such data as he receives from reliable sources, while the fact still remains that much valuable and reliable data never reach him. This is largely due to our defective system of procuring authentic information in reference to our nation's annual productive capacity. Unofficial and yet most reliable information is before this office showing very material increases over the reported yields of some of the States as collected by the statistical bureau.

OREGON AND THE LOUISIANA PURCHASE.

Having digressed thus far to show the profitableness of our Oregon and Mexican acquisitions, I return to conclude the consideration of the American claim to the Oregon country so far as to prove that our title could not be deduced through the Louisiana Purchase.

Mr. Calhoun, Secretary of State, in presenting the claims of the United States to the Oregon country, relied, he said, upon "our own proper claims and those we have derived from France and Spain. We ground the former as against Great

Britain on priority of discovery and priority of exploration and settlement." Referring to our claims derived from France under the Louisiana Purchase, he said:

> It also added much to the strength of our title to the r⸺ beyond the Rocky Mountains by restoring to us the important link of contiguity westward to t... ific, which had been surrendered by the treaty of 1763. * * * It is therefore not at all surp... g that France should claim the country west of the Rocky Mountains (as may be inferred from ... ups) on the same principle that Great Britain had claimed and dispossessed her of the regions w... the Alleghany. * * * But since then we have strengthened our title by adding to our prop... ims and those of France the claims also of Spain by the treaty of Florida. The claims which w... acquired from her between the Rocky Mountains and the Pacific rest on her priority of discove...

These extracts from Mr. Calhoun's argument exhibit in brief his reasoning for connecting the Louisiana cession with the country west of the Rocky Mountains. It will be observed that it is largely confined to the claim of contiguity. He does not pretend that the country was originally included in the cession, except as he refers to France having claimed that country; and it will be noticed that he only infers this from French maps. The answer to this inference is that but very few French maps, as a matter of fact, ever showed that country as belonging to France, through Louisiana. The first French maps after La Salle's discovery and after the naming of Louisiana by him, excluded the country beyond the mountains from Louisiana.

The fact that Mr. Calhoun was compelled to resort to inference to establish a claim is rather presumptive of his own doubt, and when we notice his further admission that we "strengthened our title" by adding the claims of Spain west of the Rockies, his doubt is doubly shown. He further sanctions the claims of Spain when he refers to the priority of Spanish discoveries in the Pacific, as he quotes from history, and cites the voyages of the Spanish navigator, Maldonado, in 1528, ending with those under Galiano and Voldes in 1792, all being under the authority of Spain and all fruitful in discovery upon the Pacific coast. He says—

> That they discovered and explored not only the entire coast of what is now the Oregon territory, but still farther north, are facts too well established to be controverted at this day.

He further mentions the discovery of the mouth of the Columbia prior to Captain Gray's discovery, and refers to it as the "incontestable claim to the discovery of the mouth of the river by Heceta." No facts are presented tending to show that Louisiana extended so far west.

In his second argument, or reply, he again declares that the claim of the United States "rests in the first place on priority of discovery sustained by their own proper claims and those derived from Spain through the treaty of Florida." He makes his strong point against the British claim, and in favor of our own, when in his reply, he reminds the English negotiator of the latter's fatal admission in his argument, conceding that Heceta, August 15, 1775, was the first to discover the mouth of the Columbia River; he further reminds the Englishman "that Captain Gray was the first to pass its bar, enter its mouth, and sail up its stream."

Mr. Calhoun in this reply, while outlining some what more clearly what he means by "contiguity" as a claim through the Louisiana cession, by coupling that claim with our purchase of Louisiana, admits that France never claimed Louisiana as extending beyond the Rockies, when, in referring to the French claim, he said the right of France to Louisiana extended "to the region drained by the Mississippi and its waters, on the ground of settlement and exploration." It is difficult to conceive how, on such a basis, France could deduce a claim, through contiguity, to a country so remote and separated by such physical obstacles as the great Rocky Mountain range.

THE CLAIM OF CONTIGUITY.

A claim west of the Rockies, through our purchase of Louisiana, by reason of contiguity is especially untenable, because the western limit of Louisiana was sufficiently definite, it being known that the highlands at the head of the Mississippi and its tributary waters constituted the boundary. The claim of contiguity most often arises where there is uncertainty as to limit. In the case of the discovery and exploration of a river it extends to the country drained by that river. This being determined as the accepted rule, what reasoning can justify a claim for an excess of territory on the ground of contiguity? Especially is it difficult to reconcile such claim with justice where such excess is adversely claimed, as in the case of Spain to the country west of the Rockies, based on quite good showing of long prior discovery and partial settlement. If contiguity is to be applied, then, on this basis Spain would be preferred, since her acknowledged possession and dominion of the California country brought the Oregon country to the north at least far more contiguous to her possessions than it was to the country occupied in the Louisiana cession. The nations of the earth very promptly repudiated Spain's claim to the whole of the western continent, based on her early discoveries of a small portion. England, France and Portugal were likewise denied recognition of claims to vast regions on the same ground. The British did not claim extension of territory from Hudson Bay on the ground of contiguity; they justified their extension by right of exploration and discovery; this claim, though denied by our nation, had much to do in the final adjustment of the British boundary, not only in the recognition by Russia of Britain's claim south of 54° 40′, but by our own negotiators and countrymen in at last agreeing that the line between the British and American possessions should be along the forty-ninth parallel. Mr. Calhoun admits that the claim of Spain to the entire continent, on the ground of contiguity, by reason of discovery by Columbus, was not acquiesced in by other nations. He also admits that it is an abstract question how far a claim by contiguity can extend beyond the precise spot discovered or occupied, and that "it is subject in each case to be influenced by a variety of considerations." Accepting this qualification, it may be submitted, then, that in the case of the western boundary of the Louisiana cession, a very strong and conclusive consideration, precluding any further contention, is the admitted fact that so well known a physical obstruction as the great Rocky Mountain range st⎯⎯ is a barrier to the west, and forms the highlands from which are drained the wa⎯⎯ lowing into the Mississippi, the discovery of which constitutes the French c⎯⎯ to the country east of the Rocky Mountains. Can it not be said when a claim⎯⎯ based on discovery of the mouth of a river, that the further claim of contigui⎯⎯ rom the precise spot discovered is limited to and fully met by including all t⎯⎯ country drained by that river and its tributaries? That Mr. Calhoun did not a⎯⎯ h much importance to his contiguity argument in his able presentation of our n⎯⎯ on's claim, is evident from his reply to the British plenipotentiary, when he sa⎯⎯ "The cession of Louisiana gave us undisputed title west of the Mississippi, ex⎯⎯ ding to the summit of the Rocky Mountains, and south, between that river and tho⎯⎯ mountains, to the possessions of Spain." Mr. Buchanan, as Secretary of State⎯⎯ following Mr. Calhoun, at the point left off by him, relied but little on the contiguity claim, as he announced that—

> The title of the United States to that portion of the Oregon territory between the valley of the Columbia and the Russian line in 50° 40′ north latitude *is recorded in the Florida treaty*. Under this treaty, dated on the 22d of February, 1819, Spain ceded to the United States all her rights, claims, and pretensions to any territories west of the Rocky Mountains and north of the forty-second parallel of latitude. We contend that at the date of this cession Spain had a good title, as against Great Britain, to the whole Oregon territory.

The view I here submit as to the doctrine of contiguity is approved in Lawrence's Principles of International Law, page 152, which holds that—

> In the absence of natural features, the boundary of the contiguous settlements of two States should be drawn midway between the last posts on either side. * * * But there can be no doubt that natural boundaries would be preferred to an imaginary line, in cases where they exist.

The same authority admits that the rights of sovereignty gained by occupation may extend beyond the actual place inhabited, but, it adds, "the reasonable doctrine of expansion must not be pushed to absurd lengths." Modern international law does not sanction Mr. Calhoun's contiguity claim as he endeavored to extend it, nor have I found any authority that ever did.

Pomeroy's International Law, page 105, declares that—

> It is evident that those natural boundaries which physical geography points out—the ranges of mountains, the great rivers draining large basins, the gulfs and bays, the prominent capes, and the trend of the coast line—must have great influence in determining the limits of national domain.

A claim of contiguity is sufficiently met by conceding to the nation under whose flag the mouth of a river is discovered all the country drained by that river; otherwise a nation would be restricted to the precise spot on which its people first landed or settled. To claim beyond the drainage of the river, on the theory of contiguity, would be as unjust and unreasonable as to limit possession by actual occupancy. These are two extremes.

The contiguity claim of Calhoun in reference to the Louisiana Purchase was not approved by Monroe and Pinckney, the American negotiators at Madrid in 1803-1805, where the question of territorial extent following discovery was discussed. They contended that—

When any European nation claims possession of any extent of seacoast, that possession is understood as extending into the interior country to the sources of the rivers emptying within that coast, to all their branches, and the country they cover.

These views constitute the recognized international doctrine of contiguity, and, as so held, Mr. Calhoun's attempt to claim Oregon through the Louisiana Purchase by virtue of contiguity can not be sustained.

It has been asserted by some that the British claim to the Pacific Northwest was defended on the ground of contiguity, based upon the English right to the Hudson Bay country. Such, however, is not the fact.

SIR ALEXANDER McKENZIE'S EXPEDITION.

The first exploration of the continent, and the first success in discovering a route by land from ocean to ocean, was that by Alexander McKenzie and party, and many of the names they gave to rivers and mountains along their memorable journey remain to-day to remind us of the intrepid men who achieved this great triumph. Two years after his voyage down the McKenzie river to its entrance into the Arctic Ocean, and on his return to Fort Chepewyan on Ithabasca Lake, McKenzie, on the 10th day of October, 1792, started in a birch-bark canoe with a few fellow-voyagers on his search of a route to another remote point on the great Pacific Ocean. He followed up the Peace river as far as possible to a point in longitude 121°, and then crossing the summit of the mountains came upon the waters flowing toward the Pacific; which he thought to be the Columbia river, as Fraser also thought when he saw it thirteen years later, and to which he subsequently gave his name as it is now known, Fraser river, but which was then known by the natives as the Tacootche. Over rapids and through narrow and tortuous channels, the descending waters broadened and spread until they formed a large-sized river which McKenzie followed to a point near the junction of the Blackwater, or, as he names it on his map, the West Road River; and there he turned his course more directly to the west, and on the morning of the 20th of July, 1793, the great object of his journey being accomplished, he floated on the tide waters of the Pacific Ocean. Proceeding southwesterly he reached Point Menzes on the coast, shown by Vancouver on his map, and then exploring the Burke and Dean canals he journeyed up the Cascade canal; all of which the British navigator had surveyed but two months before McKenzie reached his last point, and there, standing above the waves of the Pacific, he painted on a rocky cliff overhanging the seashore, in memory of his great exploit, these words: "Alexander Mackenzie, from Canada by land the twenty-second of July, one thousand seven hundred and ninety-three."

This early claim the British united with their other claims by virtue of coast discoveries, and their much stronger claim through the Nootka Sound Convention of 1790, wherein they claimed that Spain had ack...wledged their right to joint occupancy and settlement; and they relied on t... rather than through contiguity to Hudson Bay.

This Nootka claim was resisted by our negoti...ors, who insisted that this right was merely transient and did not interfere with Spain's exclusive sovereignty, and that, whatever that right was, it was annulled by the war between Spain and Britain in 1796. Yet, with all this, the claim was of great weight with the negotiators in conceding to Britain the territory lying north of the forty-ninth parallel.

NO PROOF THAT OREGON WAS INCLUDED IN THE LOUISIANA PURCHASE.

It is noticeable in all the authorities asserting the Louisiana Purchase to extend beyond the Rocky Mountains to the Pacific that no substantial support is found for such assumption of fact. In the American additions to Chambers Encyclopedia the assertion is made that Idaho, Oregon and Washington were embraced within the Louisiana territory. No authority or reason is given for such statement.

In Guthrie's Universal Geography, Volume I, the statement is made that the limits of Louisiana extended to the Pacific Ocean. No proof accompanies this assertion.

Russell's History of the United States claims that the cession included "not only Louisiana but the whole country from the Mississippi to the Pacific." It is satisfied with this mere assertion.

Olney's History of the United States contains two sentences in reference to the same claim, ending with the bare assertion: "as it included all that part of the country west of the Mississippi, extending to Mexico and the Pacific Ocean." Other histories are equally deficient in proof where the same statement is made.

OFFICIAL DECLARATION INCREASED POPULAR ERROR.

Perhaps no publication in late years contributed so much in confirming such erroneous statements as did the official declaration made in the census reports of 1870.

The report of that census contains a map which represents the present area of Oregon, Washington and Idaho as having been included in and acquired through the Louisiana Purchase of 1803. Coming with this official sanction of the government, it has been adopted by the public as a declaration to be relied on. Following that report was the publication of the Public Domain, prepared pursuant to acts of Congress approved March 3, 1879, and June 16, 1880. This contained a map on the plan of the census map, and was an acquiescence in the error of the census report as to this subject. Since then various historians have accepted the statement as an historic truth and it has been taught in the schools of the country. The present map, as published by the Interior Department, and which is to be corrected in this respect in a new publication, is copied from and justified by the map which is made a part of the Ninth Census and by the "Public Domain." This office merely followed that authority. Gen. F. A. Walker, the superintendent of that census, when called upon to justify his official representation, replied that, as he recalled the negotiations, our government made claim to Oregon by virtue of the Louisiana Purchase. Subsequently, when again asked by a leading educator his reasons for representing the extension beyond the Rocky Mountains, he answered: "I am free to confess that my individual views do not coincide therewith." Prof. John J. Anderson, Ph.D., a well-known author of many historical publications, and of a widely used school history of the United States, in an able contribution, entitled, "Did the Louisiana Purchase extend to the Pacific Ocean?" sums up his conclusions by saying:

> Nowhere have we seen any attempt whatever to prove that any part of the region west of the Rocky Mountains ever belonged to France, or that France ever made any pretense of conveying it to the United States. It was no part of the Louisiana Purchase.

McMaster's History of the people of the United States," [Volume 2, page 633] expresses substantially the same view in the following language:

> Never at any time did Oregon form part of Louisiana. Marbois denied it, Jefferson denied it. There is not a fragment of evidence in its behalf. Our claim to Oregon was derived, and derived solely from the Florida Treaty of 1819, the settlement at Astoria, the explorations of Lewis and Clark, and the discovery of the Columbia river by Robert Gray.

Commenting upon the same error in the present General Land Office map of the United States, Col. James O. Broadhead, of St. Louis, a distinguished American statesman and scholar, in a recent lecture delivered before the Missouri Historical Society, entitled, "The Louisiana Purchase: Extent of Territory Acquired by the Purchase," very critically reviews the leading authorities upon this subject, and expresses his own judgment by saying that all these sources of information "establish beyond a reasonable doubt the fact that by the treaty of 1803 the territory ceded by France to the United States embraced only the territory watered by the Mississippi and Missouri rivers and their tributaries."

JEFFERSON, MARBOIS, AND GREENHOW.

If there were no other proofs as to the Louisiana cession not extending westward of the Rocky Mountains the declarations of three men alone should be conclusive; they are those of Jefferson, the President of our Republic, who did so much to accomplish the cession; Marbois, minister of France, who earnestly seconded Napoleon's desire to cede; and Greenhow, the historian, who perhaps gave to the subject more exhaustive study than any other man. Greenhow was librarian of the State Department of the United States, and prepared a most comprehensive report to Congress on the subject, and at a time when every contribution relating to the discussion was closely read. He also published a history of California and Oregon, in which he reviews this subject of the Louisiana cession.

President Jefferson's instructions through Mr. Madison, his Secretary of State, to Monroe and Pinckney, July 30, 1807, expressed and explained the terms on which they were directed to close the treaty, and contains this language as to boundaries:

This is in no view whatever necessary, and can have little other effect than as an offensive intimation to Spain that our claims extend to the Pacific Ocean. However reasonable such claims may be compared with others, it is impolitic, especially at the present moment, to strengthen Spanish jealousies of the United States, which it is probably an object with Great Britain to excite by the clause in question.

Another statement from Mr. Jefferson—and four years earlier—is in his letter to Mr. Breckenridge, which I subjoin in full, so far as it refers to the Louisiana boundaries:

To Mr. BRECKENRIDGE.
MONTICELLO, *August 12, 1803*.

DEAR SIR,—The enclosed letter, though directed to you, was intended to me also, and was left open with a request, that when forwarded, I would forward it to you. It gives me occasion to write a word to you on the subject of Louisiana, which being a new one, an interchange of sentiments may produce correct ideas before we are to act on them.

Our information as to the country is very incomplete; we have taken measures to obtain it full as to the settled part, which I hope to receive in time for Congress. The boundaries, which I deem not admitting question, are the highlands on the western side of the Mississippi enclosing all its waters, the Missouri, of course, and terminating in the line drawn from the northwestern point of the Lake of the Woods to the nearest source of the Mississippi, as lately settled between Great Britain and the United States. We have some claims to extend on the seacoast westwardly to the Rio Norte or Bravo, and better, to go eastwardly to the Rio Perdido, between Mobile and Pensacola, the ancient boundary of Louisiana. These claims will be a subject of negotiation with Spain, and if, as soon as she is at war, we push them strongly with one hand, holding out a price in the other, we shall certainly obtain the Floridas, and all in good time. * * *

This treaty must of course be laid before both Houses.

Another letter to General Gates, about the same time, is also in point:

To General GATES.
WASHINGTON, *July 11, 1803*.

DEAR GENERAL,—I accept with pleasure, and with pleasure reciprocate your congratulations on the acquisition of Louisiana; for it is a subject of mutual congratulation, as it interests every man of the nation. The territory acquired, as it includes all the waters of the Missouri and Mississippi, has more than doubled the area of the United States, and the new parts is not inferior to the old in soil, climate, productions and important communications. * * *

Marbois, in his History of Louisiana, referring to the extent of the Louisiana cession, says:

The shores of the western ocean were certainly not included in the cession, but the United States are already established there. (See p. 286.)

Marbois again says:

The charter given by Louis XIV to Crozat included all the countries watered by the rivers which empty directly or indirectly into the Mississippi. Within this description comes the Missouri, a river that has its sources and many of its tributary streams at a little distance from the Rocky Mountains. The first article of the treaty of cession to the United States meant to convey nothing beyond them, but the settlement in the interior, which has resulted from it, and the one on the Pacific Ocean at the west have mutually strengthened each other. (See p. 291.)

Greenhow, in his History of California and Oregon, commenting on the boundaries of the Louisiana Purchase, says:

> In the absence of more direct light on the subject from history we are forced to regard the boundaries indicated by nature -namely, the highlan separating the waters of the Mississippi from those flowing into the Pacific or the California Gulf as the true western boundaries of the Louisiana ceded by France to Spain in 1762, retroceded to France in 1800, and transferred to the United States by France in 1803.

France, at the time of the cession, did not claim any territory west of the Rocky Mountains, but did concede the dominion of Spain to that country, as Spain then, and before, claimed the same. In support of this assertion we have the official declaration of Talleyrand, the French minister, to the Spanish Government (August 31, 1804, Talleyrand to Gravine), as follows:

> In any case the Court of Madrid would have no ground for the fear it shows that the United States may make use of their possession of Louisiana in order to form possessions on the northwest coast of America. Whatever boundary may be agreed upon between Spain and the United States, the line will necessarily be so far removed from the western coast of America as to relieve the Court of Madrid from anxiety on that score.

These evidences from the highest and most authentic sources, and these expressions from men who lived in the times when this great question was most closely and critically examined, constitute the best authority, and should be finally and forever conclusive upon the controversy as to the extent of the Louisiana Purchase.

Having reached this conclusion as to the western boundary of the cession from France history equally justifies us in our claim to the Oregon country to the westward of the cession, now embracing the States of Oregon, Washington and Idaho, and portions of Montana and Wyoming as resting on and derived through—

First. Discovery and entrance of the mouth of the Columbia River by Capt. Robert Gray in 1792.

Second. Exploration by Lewis and Clarke in 1805.

Third. Settlement and occupation by the Astoria party in 1811.

Fourth. Relinquishment of the rights of Spain by the treaty of 1819.

Therefore the Cession Map of the United States should be made to conform to facts well established and long confirmed by history, with which, I respectfully submit, the position assumed in this review of the question is in complete accord.

A REVIEW OF ANNEXATION BY THE UNITED STATES.

EARLY OBJECTIONS TO ANNEXATION ANALYZED.

Annexation and affiliation within the confines of the great American Republic have become the popular thought of the people inhabiting the countries adjoining or near our shores. There is a magnetism about the old flag which attracts these people to us. It means to them freedom and humanity. It means greater opportunities. This was the feeling in Florida, in Texas, in California and in Oregon. Eighteen great States and four prosperous Territories and Districts, with Hawaii, comprise the domain acquired by annexation from foreign powers—vastly exceeding in area that wrested from our British ancestors by the Revolutionary war—and all within the lifetime of many still living.

There are in the present American Congress 24 Senators and 65 Representatives from States within the limits of the Louisiana Purchase; from this, and our other foreign acquisitions, there are to-day in that Congress 40 Senators and 97 Representatives and Delegates. Though innumerable advantages have accrued to our nation by territorial expansion, and though we have become greater and stronger with each increase of our area and acquired population, yet every effort to expand our domain has been antagonized by many of our own people. Some very specious arguments, as hereinbefore shown, have been advanced in opposition, but the experience of our nation during many years enable us now to refute the different positions assumed.

Remoteness.—The objection to cession of foreign territory especially because of remoteness has been urged in the past to all our accessions. That this has neither resulted to the injury of our union nor to our institutions we have evidences all around us. We observe that Hawaii is more accessible to the United States to-day than were the settled portions of Louisiana in Jefferson's time, or of Florida in that of Monroe, and indeed nearer, as well as more accessible, than was Oregon during Polk's administration. To the answer that these acquisitions were neither interrupted by foreign dominion, nor by oceans, we turn to Alaska. We find that District not only incontiguous, but separated by a foreign country. It is also a fact that all communication with that distant people and with our civil government there is by ocean; the distance from Seattle to Sitka by steamer or sailing vessel being 900 miles, and from Seattle to St. Michaels, at the mouth of the Yukon, it is 2,705 miles. Hawaii is nearer the American mainland than are some of our Aleutian Islands. California when admitted into the Union was far more inaccessible than is Hawaii to-day. Gen. Joseph ———, the first Territorial governor of Oregon, desired to reach that destination as early as possible, so as to proclaim the Federal authority over that Territory before the expiration of President Polk's term, on March 4, 1849. He departed with his commission from Indiana on August 27, 1848, and journeyed via Fort Leavenworth, Santa Fe, El Paso, and thence to California, where at San Pedro Bay he took passage on a sailing vessel and was conveyed to San Francisco. Here, finding a ship bound for the Columbia river, he was transported to Oregon, where he arrived on the 1st of March following—the journey occupying about six months!

President Polk, in a message to Congress, thought it might be practicable to establish an overland mail once a month, and so advised.

Now, this distance is traversed in five days with comfort and safety, and for reasonable compensation. By our modern contrivances time, distance and danger are largely overcome in transportation from point to point. The wagon and the stage-coach are distanced and surpassed by the steam car; the sail has for quick dispatch given way to steam; the wooden vessel has been supplanted by the iron ship; and expedition in communication and correspondence between individuals is accomplished through the fast mail, the telegraph, and the telephone.

THE CONSTITUTIONALITY OF ANNEXATION.

The doubt entertained as to the right under the Constitution to acquire possession of foreign territory has been answered by the several acquisitions made since that of Louisiana, as well as by the judgments of the highest courts and in the opinions and writings of our most illustrious jurists. Chief Justice Marshall, rendering the opinion of the Supreme Court of the United States in the case of The American Insurance Company v. Canter, said:

> The Constitution confers absolutely on the Government of the Union the power of making wars and making treaties, consequently the Government possesses the power of acquiring territory either by conquest or treaty.

The Supreme Court again, in another celebrated case, The Mormon Church v. The United States (136 U. S. R.), said:

> The power of acquiring territory is derived from the treaty-making power and the power to declare and carry on war. * * * The antecedents of these powers are those of national sovereignty, and belong to all independent governments.

The further provision of the Constitution conferring on Congress the power to provide for the common defense and to promote the general welfare implies also the authority, when necessary, to acquire territory. It is a power inherent in the fundamental nature of government, and involves a principle of maintenance, of defense, of perpetuity.

There have been many Executive interpretations of the Constitution in consonance with these views in treaties through which we acquired the larger part of our domain, and in several other treaties negotiated for foreign territory, which were never consummated by ratification, such as Hawaii in 1854, Santo Domingo in 1870, Hawaii again in 1893, and still later in 1897. Congress has also given its assent to the doctrine at different times in our history. Having thus the acceptance of the executive, the legislative, and the judicial departments of the government, it should now be regarded as an established right.

ANNEXATION AN ELEMENT OF STRENGTH.

To the argument used as to annexation being a source of weakness, our experience has proven it to be an element of strength. As bases of supply in war time we have been taught that many of our accessions have been invaluable. Our great battle ships are propelled by steam, and coal for fuel is indispensable. Bases of supply must be had. Our warships crossing the ocean, or distant from the mainland, and with exhausted coal bunkers meeting the enemy will invite destruction. Stress of weather, disabled machinery, or other accidents produce delay. If relief is sought in neutral ports they will be closed against the ship's necessities except under certain restrictions. Modern invention has given rise to this necessity for fuel supply. In former years our ships of war were propelled by wind and sail, and a distant base of supply was a matter of comparative indifference. Outlying points overlooking the mainland, or in the track of our commerce, afford means for defensive operations in time of need which no nation should disregard. Territorial defense, protection against military or naval attack, and avoidance of conflict with numerous adjoining powers are advantages which we have gained through annexation.

The nations of the Old World are in frequent disputes and sometimes wars arising over boundary disputes, customs violations, and clash of jurisdictions, requiring large standing armies to resist invasion or to punish real or fancied wrongs.

International complications rarely occur with us because of our immunity from such elements of discord and the legion of controversies which originate among close neighbors having rival interests. Our brief experience with Florida and with Louisiana when under Spanish control gave us an object lesson of the effect of undesirable neighbors. Territorial expansion may, therefore, be justified as a war measure as well as upon grounds of commercial necessity.

HOMOGENEITY NOT A SERIOUS OBJECTION.

To the further objection that the populations of annexed foreign territory are not homogeneous with our own, we have discovered from experience that this is no serious objection in the end. In all of our cessions we have had a mixture of races to contend with. With Florida we acquired a Spanish and Indian population; with Texas the Spaniard, the Mexican, and the Indian; with California the same; with Louisiana we had the Spaniard, the Frenchman, and the Indian, and with Alaska we had the Russian and the Eskimo.

It has in all cases been demonstrated that the stronger races dominate. The American element proves in every contest for supremacy to be the stronger. It is a great colonizer and educates as it advances. Wherever it goes our institutions go with it. Before it the foreign element becomes Americanized in a brief period. It is a formidable missionary.

A further check is provided against possible danger of racial conflict or lack of homogeneity in the population—so far as the purposes of our civil form of government may be perverted by the participation in its affairs of elements alien and antagonistic—in the exclusion of such elements from the exercise of governmental functions. They are never at the time of accession admitted or accepted as citizens with political rights. When they shall enjoy such privileges is a matter which is left entirely with Congress. In the meanwhile they are required to undergo a probation or pupilage which in the course of time will fit them to become the guardians of republican institutions. A long period may intervene before they may be allowed to enjoy a territorial form of government, with its restricted privileges, and thereafter a still longer period may ensue before statehood will follow to confer the highest rights of citizenship. A perpetual check is thus provided by the Constitution against the incorporation into our political system of state or national government of an element unfitted to control. To argue that this restraint is insufficient or may be disregarded is to reflect upon the intelligence, the integrity, and the patriotism of the people's representatives in the Congress of all the States of our Union. Of this Congress is the best judge, and can always be depended upon when to admit these territorial accessions into the Union as States, and thus far this high trust has been discharged with eminent satisfaction and discretion. No Territory will be admitted into the Union until the people shall have demonstrated their capacity for statehood, and, even when admitted, Congress can legislate such limitations and restrictions as shall best conserve the public interests, as it can exclude and prohibit any undesirable people from becoming residents of our country.

ANNEXATION BY OTHER NATIONS AND THEIR FOREIGN ELEMENTS.

The adoption of different racial elements in the body politic is the history of the ages. All nations have gone through this ordeal. Great Britain is an appropriate illustration. She has assimilated the most diverse beings, and from the most unfavorable conditions brought them under highly enlightened and Christianizing influences; she has made them as thoroughly British in sentiment and industrial habits as the people of England themselves, and her colonial possessions are to-day the strength and glory of that great Empire. Like France, Holland and Portugal, England has more inhabitants in her colonial possessions than she has at home. At home she has 39,825,000, while in her colonies she has 322,000,000. At home France has 38,520,000, and in her colonies 44,290,000. Portugal has 5,050,000 at home and 10,215,000 in her colonies. The area of the

German Empire proper is but one-fifth that of her colonial possessions, while the area of England's colonial possessions is eighty times as great as the home country. This mere statement necessarily implies the diverse character of the races which go to make up the population of the widely scattered possessions of these nations. Nor can it be said that these mighty powers have become enervated or denationalized in spirit or threatened in unity because of their annexations or distant colonial possessions.

AN OBJECT LESSON IN ENGLAND'S ASSIMILATION OF RACES.

An illustration as forcible as it was beautiful of the success in the cementing and assimilating of Britain's widely different colonial elements was witnessed in the city of London the past year at the Queen's Jubilee in commemoration of the sixtieth anniversary of her reign. There were assembled in the mighty concourse present representatives from each of the British colonies who came to do honor and to express their fealty to the great head of the consolidated Empire. As an object lesson of the strength of the several remote possessions, their military was most conspicuous in the magnificent cavalcade. Troops were there from Canada, India, New South Wales, Hongkong, Cape Colony, Jamaica, New Zealand, Australia, and other portions of the English domain—in all, the military of twenty-five colonies were in the march. The native troops were there. The black and the bronzed faces proclaimed their racial status. Some wore the fez, some the red cap, some the gay colored turban, some the Chinese head covering, and so on, while the uniforms displayed were even more varied in style and color. There were exhibited the same proud tread in the movements and the same loyal devotion in the faces of the dragoons of Manitoba, the infantrymen of the West Indies, the hussars and lancers of New South Wales, and the North Borneo policemen, as were seen in the Royal Dragoons of London.

As showing the wealth, strength and power which have come to Great Britain through annexation within Queen Victoria's reign, it will be of interest to read the recent comments of Gen. Nelson A. Miles, of the United States Army (see McClure's Magazine for July, 1898), upon the secret of England's mighty prestige. He says:

In 1837, when Victoria was crowned, the entire white colonial population was only 1,250,000. To-day it is over 10,000,000. At that time India was not yet a direct dependency of the Crown, but was still under the rule of the East India Company. Hongkong had not been added as a military outpost, nor was nearly so large a part of the Malay Peninsula under British control. In all Australia, in 1837, there were only about 100,000 British colonists scattered in Tasmania, New Zealand, and South Australia—and most of these were supposed to be felons and convicts. The interior of Australia was entirely unexplored. The resources were unknown, its future undreamed. To-day Australia is made up of seven rich provinces and has a population of 4,000,000 as loyal, intelligent, and progressive British subjects as exist on the globe.

In South Africa sixty years ago the English domain was confined to the southern point of the continent; to-day it extends, with only one important break, from the Cape to the sources of the Nile. When Victoria ascended the throne the British in North America were nearly all gathered in Ontario and Quebec, and the Hudson Bay Company occupied all the central and western provinces of what is now known as the Canadian Dominion. British Columbia was an unknown waste, only to be reached by a terrible sea voyage around Cape Horn. Yet to-day Imperial Government is in force over all this vast territory. London is now only ten days from Vancouver, and every year is seeing the development of new resources by a territory once believed to be useless except as a fur-producing country.

OUR FURTHER DESTINY.

When we pause to review the marvelous development and expansion of our own country since the immortal proclamation of freedom was first announced from Independence Hall, Philadelphia, and realize that but little over a century measures the interval of time during which the colossal Republic has reached a limit of forty-five great States, with several important Territories and Districts, each one of which is comparable as an equal with some nation in the old world, and all of these magnificent divisions, including Hawaii, under one flag, one constitution, and one indissoluble and glorious union, may we not indulge in prophetic thought as to the wondrous revelations which the next few years of our history must unfold? We have already become the greatest agricultural, the greatest manufacturing, and the greatest mining nation. According to Mulhall we are now the wealthiest of all the nations. We have become the second greatest commercial nation, and are rapidly approaching first place. As a military and naval power, we have made a history within the present year, which has moved the American people to the front rank before the world. What shall be the further destiny of this nation? Grand and unprecedented as has been our past, we are now emerging upon an era still more resplendent, and far superior to anything that has gone before in our history. Our horizon has broadened and increased. That which before in many things was a mere interest has now become a necessity. None can predict the mighty sweep of the present evolution. It is destiny. New domains, new responsibilities, and new demands are before us. Our possessions in the distant seas will call for such government and such international policy as was never before required in our affairs. For this reason we must rely in the future more upon our Navy. This realization has already been brought home to us and we are profiting by the lesson. Fifteen years ago we ranked twelfth in maritime strength among the nations while now we have become the fifth, if not the fourth naval power. We are also entering upon an age of competition. What protection shall our vast and growing foreign and domestic commerce receive?

OUR INCREASING COMMERCE.

The Bureau of Statistics of the Treasury Department officially assures us that the exports of our country for the year ended June 30, 1898, exceed the enormous value of $1,200,000,000. No month since last August has fallen below $95,000,000, while the exports for May last amounted to $110,239,206.

The imports for the same year exceed $600,000,000 in value. It can now be said that our exports are double in value to our imports. We are selling twice as much as we are buying—a most inspiring spectacle—and a result as commendable and significant in the affairs of a nation as in those of an individual. I have

NIIHAU
Area 90
Sq. Miles.

KAUAI
Area 500
Sq. Miles
ANAHOLA
WAILEALE
5000
MAKAHUENA
Puen Pt

1,000 Miles to Yokahama

KAULA

KAIEIE WAHO CHANNEL

OAHU
Area 530
Sq. Miles.
Kahuka
LAIE
Kaena Pt
Kaneo
MON
PEARL HARBOR
HONOLULU
K. IIW

5,570 Miles to Hong Kong

5202 Miles to Manila

PACIFIC

5,200 Miles to Sydney

4400 Miles to Auckland

Compiled and dian by F.P.Houyh

Map of
HAWAII
Area, 6,049 Sq

Map of the
HAWAIIAN ISLANDS.
6,040 Square Miles.

Distances given are in Statute Miles.

2,390 Miles to San Francisco
2,000 Miles to New York, via Nicaragua Canal
5,900 Miles to Callao
6,800 Miles to Valparaiso
1,221.5 Miles to New York, via Cape Horn

PAILOLO CHANNEL
ALENUIHAHA CHANNEL

MOLOKAI — Area 190 Sq. Miles
LANAI — Area 100 Sq. Miles
MAUI — Area 620 Sq. Miles
KAHOOLAWE — Area 60 Sq. Miles
HAWAII — Area 3,950 Sq. Miles

NAKALELE
PUUKUKUI 5,788
AWALU
MANELE
KOLE KOLE
10,032
Hauiki Head
HANA
MAUPO

Upolu Pt
Honoipu Landing
WAIPIO
KAWAIHOE
HONOKAA
MAUNA KEA 13,805
Kaehole Pt
HUALALAI 8,273
Hilo Bay
HILO
MAUNA LOA 13,675
KILAUEA 4,000
Cape Kumukahi
PUNALUU
WAIOHINU
KAALUALA
KALAE

O C E A N

found no other instance within the century when the exports of a nation have been double the imports. Indeed, it is said this record is without a parallel in the annals of the world! To maintain this splendid reputation and to excel this high standard among all nations, it is essential that we shall anticipate our further development in the near future and wisely avail ourselves of such acquisition of territory, naval and coaling stations and such advantages by treaties and commercial agreements as shall enable us not only to enlarge the scope of our export traffic and further multiply the market places for our varied, wondrous, and rapidly increasing productions, but also to protect and defend the trade which shall follow the flag.

Is the imperial domain which is now the Republic to remain content with its present advance, or is it written for the future that accession and annexation shall still further progress until we shall secure the island approaches in the Atlantic which under foreign flags and rival nations still menace the way to the Gulf ports and to the great river which carries to the markets of the world the rich commerce of many of the States of the Union?

HAWAII.

It is now already written that on the Pacific side of our Republic and along the track of our increasing and lucrative commerce with the Occident and the Orient, the islands which lie to the westward and face the California shores are ours. These aggregate in area 6,040 square miles—nearly the combined area of the States of Connecticut and Delaware. They contain the little republic which has long prospered under the stimulus of American enterprise and capital, until at last 95 per cent of its property values represent the possessions of our own kindred. As an evidence of the present commercial importance to the United States of these islands, it is of interest to note that of the $200,000,000 in value of exports since 1876, more than $180,000,000 in value came to this country; and of the $100,000,000 worth of imports by Hawaii from *all* countries during the same period about $70,000,000 worth were from the United States. In this present year the American exports to Hawaii will equal $6,000,000 as against about $1,000,000 only twenty-two years ago. It is officially estimated that her exports to the United States this year will equal in value $15,000,000, while in 1876—only twenty-two years ago—they did not much exceed $1,000,000 in value. So thoroughly American has that traffic become that already 90 per cent of the entire shipments from Hawaii comes to this country. Were we not enjoined to acquire these islands as a defense to our traffic on the Pacific as it crosses and recrosses at all hours to the Asiatic shores?

OUR ASIATIC TRADE.

Our annual trade with the Orient amounts in value to over $56,000,000. Our exports to China in 1895 were only $3,603,840 in value, while they will reach a total this year of nearly $11,000,000. Our sales to that country the present year will show an increase over those of nine years ago of over 300 per cent! Our purchases from the same country only show an increase of 35 per cent. Of our total exports to Asia we have made a gain this year more than double that of 1890 and ten times greater than that of 1870. Across the Pacific we behold nearly one-half of the world's population. We are their nearest market, and, considering only our trade interests and merchant marine, should we not exercise the utmost vigilance, not only in maintaining and extending this valuable commerce, but also in providing sufficient safeguards for the future?

THE SANDWICH ISLANDS A SAFEGUARD.

Our possession of the Sandwich Islands is a safeguard. Are they not indispensable to us as a military and naval outpost for the defense of our Pacific mainland as well as a resting place and depot of supply for our merchant ships and those of our Navy? Should not such a strategic outpost long since have been added to our domain? Have we any reason to apprehend that Hawaii will add discredit to our past record of successful annexation?

The Hawaiian people as a whole are to-day further advanced educationally, industrially and commercially, than the people inhabiting any other country at the time of its annexation or cession to our domain. Their Republic has been governed in a wise, economic and statesmanlike manner. Their resources are abundant and varied, and fully justify the assurance that, with the added stimulus which annexation will give, Hawaii will eventually become the garden spot of the world, at the same time being a defensive point and a commercial aid to our country.

All hail, then, this last acquisition to the Great Republic. What a glorious interval between Louisiana in 1803 and Hawaii in 1898. As the illustrious Thomas Jefferson, for his annexation of the empire west of the Mississippi, crowned his memory with imperishable fame, so President William McKinley has added to his renown, and forever endeared himself to his fellow-countrymen, for his safe counsels and his untiring and zealous aid in the annexation of Hawaii to our domain. Together we link the names of these two great Presidents and American annexationists—the one at the beginning of the century, the other at its close. The succeeding years will richly vindicate the present Executive in this splendid act, as the past has so gloriously verified the foresight of the sage of Monticello in his record of annexation. The year 1898 will be a precious memory to all patriotic Americans. The world will gaze upon its record in wonder and admiration. The part which Americans have acted in this year will go down the ages. It will read in the future more like fable than fact. In war and in peace our trophies are as many and as grand as they are marvelous and like revelation.

THE NICARAGUA CANAL.

The intelligent judgment of the American people, which has so often approved the past policy of our country in reference to the many splendid accessions to our domain, will not hesitate to secure still further advantages by the same wise diplomacy. This hope having now been reali... ...s to Hawaii, and the track of our immense commerce along the oceanic highw... ...s far largely protected, is there not still another important duty incumbent u... ...as, as imperative as it is essential, and which appeals to every public-spirited ... patriotic American? There is; and that duty calls for the construction of the ...aragua Canal, to be not only constructed, but owned and controlled by our ...vernment. With the canal completed, our Atlantic and Pacific seaboards wi... brought nearer together by almost 11,000 miles. In the event of war with an... ...tion this canal will bring our military and naval forces from both oceans with ...ick and safe dispatch at any threatened point along our coasts or upon our i.. ..d possessions. The very security which such an advantage would confer woul... itself often prevent conflicts, as no nation would hastily engage our country in w.r with such a safeguard and such an avenue for rapid passage and national defense. The commerce of the Atlantic as well as of the Pacific demands this interoceanic highway. A stream of traffic will pour direct from the great rivers and lakes on the one side to those on the other. The products of our country will find cheap transportation for interchange in our home markets, as well as more profitable shipment to the wider marts of the world. The mouth of the Columbia river, in a sense, will be extended to the Gulf of Mexico, and the mouth of the Mississippi to the Pacific Ocean. Our people will become more closely related. Our nation will become stronger at home and more honored abroad. When the great undertaking shall have been accomplished, it can then be said that of all achievements in our industrial development none will have contributed more to the material interests of our people than this world-famed project. While extending our already vast commerce and dominion it will also contribute to the defense, the honor, and the glory of our beloved country, and be a monument to American genius and American foresight and energy as long as time shall endure.

www.ingramcontent.com/pod-product-compliance
Lightning Source LLC
Chambersburg PA
CBHW020144170426
43199CB00010B/884